Sketches from My Past

*Women's Life Writings from Around the World*

Edited by Marilyn Yalom

# SKETCHES FROM MY PAST

*Encounters*
*with*
*India's*
*Oppressed*

A Translation of Mahadevi Varma's
*Ateet Ke Chalchitra*
by Neera Kuckreja Sohoni

Northeastern University Press   *Boston*

Northeastern University Press

Library of Congress Cataloging-in-Publication Data

Varma, Maha Devi, 1907–
    [Atīta ke cala-citra. English]
    Sketches from my past: encounters with India's oppressed / a translation of
Mahadevi Varma's Ateet ke Chalchitra by Neera Kuckreja Sohoni
        p.   cm.—(Women's life writings from around the world.)
    ISBN 1-55553-198-9:
    I. Sohoni, Neera K. (Neera Kuckreja). 1943–      II. Series.
PK2098.V3A913    1994
891'.4316—dc20
    [B]                                                          94-26786

Composed in Garamond 3 by Coghill Composition Company, Richmond, Virginia. Printed and bound by the Maple Press Company, York, Pennsylvania. The paper is 55# Sebago Antique Cream, an acid-free stock.

MANUFACTURED IN THE UNITED STATES OF AMERICA

98  97  96  95  94  5  4  3  2  1

*To my mother, who taught me to love Hindi, and to my father, who believed that the gap between languages is bridgeable*

—*Neera Kuckreja Sohoni*

# Contents

# Translator's Introduction

## I

I was barely nine when I read the story that appears as Chapter 3 in the present collection. The story leaves me as sad and disturbed today as it did then. It evokes the loneliness of a child deprived of the protective arms of a real mother. I remember crying in the dark corner of my bathroom after I had read it. I also recall giving my mother an extra-tight hug before going to bed that night.

Almost four decades later, I heard Dr. Marilyn Yalom, the editor for this memoir series and the special editor for the present translated work, describe the kind of women's writing she planned to publish. Inevitably I thought of Mahadevi Varma (1907*–1987)—an outstanding Indian woman writer ranked among the luminaries of twentieth-century Hindi literature—as a fitting addition to the series.

Born in 1907, Mahadevi had a lustrous literary career that spanned nearly half a century. A poet-writer, feminist, and nationalist, she was among the distinguished and influential thinkers of modern India. Mahadevi began writing in an age when, as a result of the Indian freedom and social reform

---

*Some scholars consider her year of birth to be 1902 but 1907 seems to be more widely accepted.

movements, thousands of middle-class women were crossing the threshold from the private to the public sphere and taking up challenging occupations. Although literary women were few, those who wrote did not shy away from openly rebelling against socially prescribed roles for women. As both Indian and Western literary critics have noted, the validity of women's experiences and the need for women to take pride in their identities were central to Mahadevi's thinking.

Her brand of feminism did not arise from theorizing about life but from personal experience. She first encountered feminism when she was barely five years old and Rama, the central character of the first chapter of this book, was hired to attend on her mother. Mahadevi recalls her stubborn insistence on being addressed by Rama as *"Raja Bhaiya,"* or "Royal Beloved Brother," because she refused to accept that a mode of address applied exclusively to boys. That insistence perhaps marked the beginning of her stubborn advocacy of equal rights for women.

Born to a conventional Hindu family in a small town in northern India, she was not reared to be a rebel or dissenter. She received a solid grounding in Indian culture and tradition from her deeply religious mother. Her father, a professor of English at a prestigious college, was greatly influenced by the reform movements of the time and believed that all his children needed to be educated regardless of sex. He therefore engaged tutors to teach the young Mahadevi. Nevertheless, as child marriage was fairly common, Mahadevi found herself married at age nine. Since it was customary for the married girl to move to the husband's home only after she was physically mature, Mahadevi continued to stay with her parents, who decided that she should have the benefit of further education. Thus, she was enrolled in a girls' school and college. She completed her undergraduate degree in 1929, majoring in English, Hindi, and Philosophy, and she obtained her graduate degree in Sanskrit three years later.

Rather unnaturally for her gender and social class, Mahadevi resisted the conventional destiny that had been laid out for her. Not only did she renounce her child marriage but she chose not to marry again. Whatever the compulsions—intellectual, emotional, or sexual—that prompted her decision, the fact remains that in her personal and professional evolution, that single act marked the dividing line between the *female* and the *feminist* in her.

Mahadevi used her education and her parental support not only to forge her independent identity and destiny, but also to develop an unstinting affiliation with the oppressed gender and classes. Neither in her life nor in her work could she bring herself to accept the image of woman as inevitably weak and victimized. Her education, experience, and temperament led her to an empowering vision of woman that was much more in keeping with ancient myth and legend than with the prevailing constricted view. In Hindu mythological heroines she saw unusual courage, resilience, and dutifulness, together with an independent identity. By connecting those traits with the disadvantaged but morally and psychologically empowered women who figured in her writing, she was able to revitalize Indian women. Colonial India provided a heady setting for thinking individuals to critique the notions of political and cultural subjugation and, in that context, to rediscover their roots and identities. Gender unavoidably figured in that discourse. To shape her feminist vision, Mahadevi drew freely from the writings of Indian female and male social reformists, western suffragists and Mahatma Gandhi on the one hand, and from ancient Hindu and Buddhist canonic literature on the other.

Her universalist view of life was a logical extension of that

*Introduction*

vision. Inspired by the Hindu and Buddhist perceptions of cosmic unity and affinity, she saw human beings, animals, and nature as siblings endowed with a common heartbeat, and she sought to merge the three through her work and life. Central to that merger was the experience of shared pain or empathy. To Mahadevi salvation lay in meshing one's life with universal life and one's pain with universal pain, as the waterdrop loses itself in the sea. Her effort to bond herself to the collective human psyche was the basis for her intense personal involvement with the day-to-day lives of the common folk around her. Her biographical cum autobiographical prose, exemplified by the present volume, reflects a reverent attempt to resurrect the inner dignity of the wretched of the earth.

Although most celebrated for her contribution to *Chhaya-vad,* a new school of Hindi poetry, that broke with traditional formalism and relied on symbolism to convey the agony and ecstasy of the human heart, Mahadevi wrote equally compelling prose in which she drew moving pen-portraits of the disinherited poor of India. In particular, her goal was to document the cultural situation of women and to expose the *systemic* basis for their oppression and victimization. Rather than fiction or theory, she used real-life stories to present an informed sociological analysis of the forces and institutions that shape women's lives. Through her memoir-tales, built mainly around the women she had personally encountered, she was able to connect the exploitation of her characters with the subjugation of all women—indeed, of all oppressed peoples. Her stories sprang from, and were rooted in, the entrails of human life. She did not need to rely on fiction or rhetoric to add finesse to her real-life women warriors.

Mahadevi describes what these characters represent to her in her own preface, which is included in the present volume.

xii

Elsewhere, in her preface to another translated collection of memoir-tales she states:

> During my life's journey, the incidents and individuals that influenced me have become a part of my emotional world. From time to time, in order to relive these emotions, I have written my sketches. It is beyond human capacity to bring back incidents from the past, but it is possible to rejuvenate the deep emotions generated by these incidents. . . .
>
> My memoirs are not meant to be mere detached descriptions of incidents nor reportage of my own life story or the life stories of others. Rather, they are emotional journeys begun with the purpose of recreating those moments in which I shared and lived the feelings and experiences of others. . . .
>
> The characters found in my memoirs are outwardly simple people and helpless creatures, but on a deeper level they can be seen as symbols of eternal and primordial truths.*

## I I

The fact that Mahadevi wove her memoirs around other people's lives rather than her own made her inclusion in this series tantalizing. Relying on the allegoric technique of *Chhayavad,* Mahadevi learned to express herself in poetry indirectly and metaphorically. It was therefore natural that in prose, too, she should present herself obliquely, as a decentered protagonist.

Clearly her capacity to agonize over—and to celebrate—the human spirit is nowhere more compelling than in her recollective prose sketches, titled in the original Hindi, *Ateet Ke*

---

*Mahadevi Varma, in Preface to *Smriti ki Rekhayen,* trans. Srivastava and Srivastava (London: Peter Owen, Ltd., 1975), pp. 7–8.

*Introduction*

*Chalchitra,* or *Sketches from My Past.* To the pen-portrait she drew of Rama, the real-life Jeeves who is the basis for Chapter 1, other precious literary memorials were added from time to time. These appeared in print individually as they were composed. In 1941 the collection of eleven recollective stories was first published in book form, and it is on the eighteenth edition of that work that this translated volume is based.

My choice of this particular work for translation is conditioned very much by my interest in presenting Mahadevi as a *feminist* and an *activist.* Her poetry and its romantic mysticism brought her endless accolades; her literary writing won her a lasting place among the key exponents of Hindi literature. But her feminist life and prose are highlighted less commonly. In a modest way, this book can help fill that gap. The stories that unfold here present her as a person endowed with life vision: one who was capable of giving a face to the faceless and nameless multitudes—be it the lonely orphan girl, Binda, victimized by her stepmother (Chapter 3); the young widow about to be abandoned by her relatives because of her refusal to give up her out-of-wedlock child (Chapter 6); the child widow, Bhabhi, barred from any contact with the outside world and emotionally and physically brutalized for fear of potential wantonness (Chapter 2); or women like the tribal Lachhama (Chapter 11), the low-caste Sabiya (Chapter 4), and Radhiya (Chapter 10), who used their courage, forbearance, and magnanimity to cope with male infidelity and other ironies or vicissitudes of a patriarchal culture and a below-subsistence life.

Mahadevi used words to resurrect human lives. And she told the human saga in all its truth and without compromise. Her stories are moral allegories. The eleven carefully crafted and dramatically powerful tales have important ethical lessons that speak through the events and characters rather than

xiv

through the narrator. Although the narrative is interspersed with occasional moral discourse by the author, the impact or flow of the stories is rarely disrupted. The moral themes unfurl through the actions and fates of the protagonists rather than through the author's statement—and thus, the stories are moralistic without being sententious.

## III

Concern about Mahadevi's ideological "softness" surfaces regularly among Hindi literary critics as well as among Indian feminists. The most common criticism is that she does not take an ideological stance: in her memoir-tales and other writing, the "class enemy" is not identified. Looking for Marxist or other designated dialectic in Mahadevi is like searching for mathematical theorems in an art book. Such an approach discards the value of sentiment, realism, and universalism—the three pillars on which Mahadevi constructed her empathetic and activist literary style. It also places too much value on the doctrinaire.

Another charge frequently levied against Mahadevi is that not only does she shy away from the moral responsibility to identify the "class enemy" but she offers no solutions to the "woman question." In response, I can do no better than to quote an old Chinese proverb:

Birds do not sing because they have answers;
Birds sing because they have songs.*

Evidence of Mahadevi's activist leanings is amply apparent in the way she dealt with the unfortunate both in her discourse

*A. K. Ramanujan, quoted in Preface to *Folktales from India* (New Delhi: Viking, 1993), p. xii.

and in her day-to-day life. Like some literary critics, I sub-
scribe to the belief that Mahadevi shows not only compassion
for the exploited class but also immense rage at those who
exploit. The voice of a rebel resonates throughout her prose.
Through the medium of the marginalized and the oppressed,
she gives expression to her compassion as well as insurrection.
Moreover, Mahadevi's compassion and empathy do not end
with the creation of poignant literary pieces about the oppressed. She does not take the easy way out to resolve her
"class" or "individual" guilt. On the contrary, by taking the
oppressed into her protective care, as with the characters in
Chapter 6, she brings new meaning to their lives. This is
irrefutable evidence that she is no armchair analyst or passing
observer of life's tragedies but a writer who seeks activist
solutions to people's pressing problems. In one of her works,
Mahadevi notes that the thought that is born in her mind
finds it necessary to express itself in action. Clearly her writing
is not separate from her life view or her life-style.

## IV

Speaking through a translator is never easy. It is
even less so when the voice is as complex as Mahadevi's. Her
language is poetic and prolific, mostly ornate, occasionally
even cumbersome, but rarely outdated. Mahadevi herself has
noted the complex delicacy of the translator's task:

> The work of a translator is more difficult than the work of the
> writer herself because she has the task of transmuting the
> living images of one language into those of another. Every
> language reflects a society's intellect and heart throughout its
> history. That is why attempting to put the ideas of one

language into another is like trying to transplant the fragrance of one flower on to another.*

Languages, like foods, carry their own ingredients and flavors. It is difficult to transplant a whole literary and cultural tradition through the medium of translation. Guided and goaded by Dr. Yalom, I have tried to make the translated text as readable and faithful as possible. Because of fundamental differences between Hindi and English, it was not always possible to render the syntax and rhythms with exactness. However, I have stayed close to the narrative and have taken care to omit no significant motif while keeping the spirit and essence of Mahadevi's writing intact.

# V

To prospective readers, I wish to make a singular appeal. To enjoy these eleven memoir-tales, you need to cross a threshold into what A. K. Ramanujan calls "another kind of cultural space" and travel within the metaphor of Mahadevi's poetic text and vision. Our aesthetic is closely linked to our culture, tradition, collective memory, time, and our understanding of creation and the cosmos—including the phenomenon of life and death. Indian perception and vision of all these concepts are distinct from the Western mind or vision. The latter is more individualistic, material, and scientistic. It is *self*-rather than *other*-centered. The Western mind seeks independence and privacy, not connectedness. What is connection to an Indian is an invasion of privacy to a Westerner. In Mahadevi's prose-pictures, there are clear

*Mahadevi Varma, in Preface to *Smriti ki Rekhayen*, p. 8.

reflections of Indian beliefs, sentiments, and relationships; cultural memory; and the Indian perception of life, death, and time.

Inevitably, both her aesthetic and moral form are characteristic of the Indian culture. Consequently, each story in these memoirs unfolds like a cultural tableau. But it is possible to transcend the cultural and literary gap through *feeling,* and with the prisms of *class* and *gender.* There is an undeniable, indelible universality in the experience of being a woman or a subaltern. Betrayal, hypocrisy arising from dual standards of morality, social control of women's sexuality, the lesser status of girls and women, and the female's exploitation and victimization are still integral to women in every setting and society. In writing about woman, patriarchal society, and the relationship of one to the other, Mahadevi transcends the borders of culture and time.

As Mahadevi perceived it, compassion unites the world as it does the reader and the writer. Although she accepted national and individual identities as natural, she saw no fundamental difference between artists and writers, whatever their nationality—whether Russian or Indian, African or American. Literature is a river, she said. In it, there are big and small waves on the surface but the river's depth is unchanged.

While historical and social contexts change, the human heart does not. When reading this book, try not to fret over the unfamiliar syntax or the alien imagery. Care to connect. Dare to be sentimental.

*28 December 1993*          NEERA KUCKREJA SOHONI
*Affiliated Scholar*
*Institute for Research on Women and Gender*
*Stanford University*
*Stanford, California*

TO

Those whose tears have cleansed my path;
Whose scattered stories have linked
   together my life's chain;
Whose affection has been pure,
   simplicity eternal, and compassion genuine;
Who are unaware of their kindnesses and
   unacquainted with my gratitude;
To those eternally vivid subjects of
   my hazy live pictures

—Mahadevi

# Author's Preface

I am unable to say anything in particular about the person to whom credit is due for these memoirs. They concern people with whom I interacted from time to time, and whose fellowship gave direction to my thinking and heightened my empathy. The anecdote I am about to relate is age-old, but one that is nonetheless soaked in pity. The mistress of a family I once knew punished her elderly servant for some petty crime by banishing him. Later, although he asked countless times to be pardoned, her arrogance did not allow her to excuse him from that baseless punishment.

Faced with that predicament, the old man, poor but rich in affection, sometimes clasping two wilted marigolds, sometimes four cookies moist with the heat of his palms, and sometimes a colorless toy, would wait at a neighboring bridge, hoping to encounter his young masters. After bestowing his humble gifts on the children as they came out for a stroll with their new servant, his eyes would fill with tears when he headed home.

Encountering that same servant in 1930, I recalled my own childhood enveloped by Rama's affection in such a compelling way that I became anxious to write the unfinished story of the past. Slowly, bit by bit, Rama's family started to expand, and to the sketches of the past, those from the present also were added. My hope was that when time, with one sweep of its brush, manages to wipe the glow off these past pictures, I may be able to resurrect them again in the hazy light of these memoirs.

I never really gave much thought to having them published. Through every intricate reflection and with each flicker of imagination, the pretty sight of the printing press did not rise before my eyes. Moreover, the subjects of these memoirs, rather than being objects of exhibition, have been the objects of my imperishable affection. Rather than test whether others would accord them similar veneration, it seemed more worthwhile to wait and defer publication.

My own life has inevitably stepped in as an integral part of these recollections. That was only natural. After all, we are able to see the objects lying in the dark only after we bring them into the dim or bright circumference of light; outside of that, they are only a part of infinite darkness. Standing within the sphere of real life, whatever self-introduction these characters are capable of giving is bound to undergo some modification as their stories are written. Nevertheless, recognizing that story writers conventionally seek to drape their fictional characters in reality to bring them closer to life, I see no reason to deliberately distance these real-life characters, who have been co-travelers on my life's path, by dressing them up in fiction. If there is an element of self-publicity in these memoirs, it is born of proximity to the characters about whom I am writing. However, it has no more significance than the ash that keeps the embers covered in an effort to keep the fire alive. Whoever is unable to recognize that my presence in these memoirs is truly incidental is not capable of reaching the heart of these sketches.

In the present collection, it has been possible to feature eleven memoir-tales. Thinking that these should provide an inexpensive source of entertainment for readers, I do not wish to treat these wounded and mauled lives as toys and put them up for sale in some toy mart. In the space of these unfinished lines and hazy colors, if someone is able to detect even a single contour of her or his reflection, then this endeavor is successful; otherwise, by bringing them out of the well-guarded limits of my memory, I have done only injustice to them.

—MAHADEVI

*Janamashtami* (Lord Krishna's Birthday) 1941
Prayaag (Allahabad, India)

Sketches from My Past

# Chapter I

Neither my brother, my sister, nor I can say precisely when Rama came and started working for us. It seems we had known him forever. He was as much a part of our childhood as father's desk, which was littered with odds and ends, and beneath which the world of our toys dwelled in the quiet of the afternoon. Rama's presence was as comforting as the huge poster bed with iron springs on which we sprawled, looking like reincarnations of Lord Vishnu as a tortoise and fish. He was as omnipresent during our childhood as the deity in Mother's prayer room, in whose solemn presence we used to stand like cranes with our eyes half shut, surrounded by conches and gongs, patiently counting each stroke of the gong while waiting to gobble up the divine sweets intended for the deity. In short, it would be fair to say that from the tips of his massive fingernails to the edge of his topknot, we had come to be fully acquainted with the short, dark-skinned, well-built Rama.

The sight of Rama's hand, with its absolutely white palm, like the underbelly of a snake, and with its fingers crooked and knotted like branches of a tree, along with every single line running across it, was all too familiar to us. This was hardly surprising since, from the moment we washed our faces early in the morning to the time he put us to bed at night, a constant state of strife existed between us, which ended only in a durable truce when we settled down to listen to him tell us bedtime stories. We had even learned to recognize the very sound of Rama's dark, massive feet: like the elders in a family, they seemed to be forever controlling the scattered clan of his toes, which appeared to travel in ten different directions. And sure enough, even when we crept on tiptoes, trying to run away silently after committing a prank, those feet managed to grow wings and chase us to our very hiding place.

There is something odd about the memories of childhood. When we are pensive and sentimental, the silhouettes from the past, like objects emerging from a fog, suddenly begin to get clearer. But when we try to be more cerebral and seek deliberately to recall past events after selectively analyzing their worth, then they tend to be overtaken by amnesia, much like the moss that temporarily divides when a stone is flung into the water, only to come back together again afterward.

Those immensely bushy eyebrows on Rama's narrow forehead and his tiny eyes, moist with affection, are sometimes imprinted on memory's screen, and at other times, they fade and disappear. The same is also true of his thick, pudgy nose, which was like the ultimate error of a tired sculptor; or of his nostrils, inflated from the flow of breathing; or of his lips, bloated from unrestrained laughter; and of a row of crowded, white teeth, reminding one of yogurt stored in a black stone bowl.

Apparently, Rama's hair was not entitled to grow more than half an inch. That is precisely why, in an effort to make it conform to its ordained length, we used to run around carrying a pair of scissors to level his topknot. But getting near that ponytail was like belling a cat: neither did its owner sleep during our waking hours nor did we dare to carry out that noble task while he was still awake! Possibly today it would have to be conceded that Rama was ugly. But at that time, even the thought that there could be a more handsome companion than Rama was unthinkable.

In reality, life is the essence of beauty. But beauty finds embodiment more readily in symmetry than in asymmetry. As we become more sophisticated and more preoccupied with appearances, we tend to lose sight of the substance of life. Unlike the adult, the child is not especially acquainted with life's coarse superficialities, which is why the child recognizes and responds only to what is sincere in life. Where the child finds rays of affection and goodwill bursting forth, it overlooks the outward disparities and differences. But where life is covered with the smoky vapor of jealousy and hatred, the child does not accept even the pretense of harmony.

It was this kind of childlike vision that made us find Rama so likeable. It seemed that Rama, too, was unaware of his ugliness. Donning just a jerkin and a loincloth that barely extended to his knees, he exhibited the greater part of his ugly form. He had no dearth of appropriate accessories; in fact, in his cabin, a long, starched shirt; a turban; shoes from the region of Bundelkhand; and a well-crafted stick seemed to be awaiting a favorable moment to be put to use. Prompted by their endless disuse and by Rama's continued indifference to them, our action committee met daily and adopted a unanimous proposal daring us to put all those precious possessions to good use. We all agreed, for instance, that by poking the walking stick through the shirt, we could create a drapelike screen for our toys; the basket-shaped turbaned headgear could be removed from its peg and given the honor of serving as a cradle for our dolls; and the Bundelkhand shoes could be dunked in the water tank to serve as a permanent form of water sport for the dolls. But Rama would frustrate all our plans by keeping his dark fortress, whose creaking door seemed to deter any visitor from coming in, locked with a

5

bolt that was placed so high we were unable to burglarize his cabin even from atop a stool.

The story of Rama's arrival, which we came to know as we grew up, is as wonderfully unique as Rama himself. One afternoon, just as Mother had laid out the imperishable treasury of salted wafers to dry in the sun, unbeknown to her, the feeble and fatigued Rama sat down on the threshold of the courtyard's door, and resting his head against the door, he virtually fainted. When Mother, taking him to be a beggar, approached and inquired if he needed anything, Rama fell at her feet saying, "Oh, Ma'am, this Rama is about to die of starvation!" Feeding him a life-restoring tonic of milk and sweets, Mother managed to revive Rama. But then the problem at hand became even more complex: afer all, hunger is not the kind of illness whose treatment can be sporadic.

Running away from his stepmother's cruelty, that rustic lad from a village in Bundelkhand had managed to reach the city of Indore by begging and eating whatever he could on the way. But in the city, he had no place to stay and no one he could call his own. Given his desperate situation, it was hardly surprising that Rama easily became the claimant of Mother's affection.

That evening when Father returned, Rama's enormous shoes were resting in one corner of the cabin where wood was stored, while his long stick stood, as if in meditation, in the other corner. Having washed his face and hands and having been inducted into his new calling as a servant, the bewildered Rama was engaged in grasping the essence and limits of his duties.

Father, of course, was completely taken aback at Rama's ugliness. Jokingly, he asked Mother, "Noble Soul! From which planet has this creature been brought?" Because of Mother's softheartedness, our house was turning into quite a

6

menagerie! Whenever Father would return from work, some
lame beggar would be having his food in the outer veranda; or
standing at the rear door, some blind person would be singing
religious songs while playing the timbrel; or occasionally some
poor child from the neighborhood, having donned a new shirt
acquired from Mother as a giveaway, would be seen racing
around the courtyard; or at times an elderly Brahman woman
would be seen at the threshold of the storehouse tying some
foodstuffs into a bundle to take home with her.

Father never showed callousness toward any of Mother's
activities, but he did derive pleasure from teasing her.

Evidently, Father had considered Rama also a momentary
guest. But feeling extremely agitated at not being able to
provide a quick and rational response to Father's question,
Mother found herself saying, "I have hired him as a special
servant to attend on me."

It was surprising enough that a person who does not rest
for even a moment, despite the presence of so many servants,
should hire a servant exclusively for herself—and such a
strange servant at that! Father laughed so much that he
practically choked. Lightheartedly, he said, "That's as it
should be. After all, only he who is molded in a special frame
that can scare away atheists is worthy of being in the good
Lord's service!"

Father could not bring himself to trust Rama, of whose
family nothing was known. But it would have been useless to
argue with Mother because she used only her intuition to
gauge a person's worthiness or unworthiness. Piercing through
Rama's outer layer of ugliness, her empathy had managed to
detect such innocence and largeheartedness that it was impossible for her to even entertain the possibility of anything other
than eternal goodness dwelling in Rama. So that is how Rama

managed to remain with us. However, the problem of defining his chores was still to be resolved.

For carrying out all the household tasks, there were already servants, and Mother was incapable of entrusting the work related to her prayer chamber and the kitchen to anyone other than herself. As inflexible and irreproachable as was Mother's routine in respect to her prayer and worship, it was no less rigid and sacrosanct when it came to cooking. On the one hand, she had faith that prayer is vital for the soul; on the other, she had the unshakable conviction that cooking the food herself was singularly necessary for the health of our bodies.

Since all of us children differed in age by only two years, there was no noticeable gap between the time when each of us moved from an age of innocence to one of maturity. Like the legendary demons perpetually engaged in disrupting religious rituals and sacrifices, we were forever hovering around to create obstructions to Mother's great undertakings. That is why, entrusting to Rama the mammoth task of keeping us insurgents under control, Mother was able to become somewhat free from anxiety.

Early in the morning, Rama would sweep the prayer chamber and scrub the prayer utensils with lemon until they sparkled. Then he would proceed to wake us up. By the time it was morning, the direction and position of our heads and feet on that massive bed would have undergone countless changes: it would appear as though someone's neck were being measured by another's foot; someone's hands had to bear the burden of another's entire body; and someone's back could be seen forming a wall choking another's breath. To assess all these situations accurately, Rama's rough hand, disguised in tenderness, would move from one end of the quilt to the other. And then, placing one of us in the carriage of his lap and another on the horseback of his shoulder, and getting yet

8

another merely to walk, Rama would transport us to participate in the important ceremony of face washing.

To get our faces and hands clean was no easy task. Rama had to chant incessantly, like a mantra, the incentive that "whoever finishes first shall be king, and milk and sugar cakes will be his!" It was evident that none of us liked having to accept another of us as the king. When Rama would address me as *Raja,* or "king," then the smallest one, opening his mouth like a bird's beak, would lisp in his childish lingo, "Lama (Rama), why do you call her Laja *(Raja)?*" The chauvinistic arrogance of that male pygmy who was not yet capable of pronouncing the letter *R* would leave me very unsettled. During the washing, my head would be stuck inside the maze-like fingers of one of Rama's hands, while the palm of his other hand, with its three thick lines, would move like Lord Krishna's deathly wheel in search of filth on my face. After enduring so much hardship, to have to accept others as claimants to kingship amounted to advertising one's own incompetence. And so, resorting to conciliation, bribery, intimidation, and divisiveness, I would compel Rama to address me alone by the title of "king." However, Rama knew the infallible mantra to console all of us brave contenders to the throne. He would whisper softly in my ear, "You alone are the grand monarch, not that little one." Possibly Rama repeated a similar whisper in my little brother's ear because, utterly elated and dipping his little finger into the box of dental powder, my brother would proceed to brush his teeth. But in his hurry to claim the right to the title of monarch, he would end us rubbing the tooth powder over his lips rather than his teeth. As that type of activity was strictly forbidden by Rama, I would look condescendingly at my little brother, as though he were a witless soldier acting in defiance of the commander-in-chief's orders.

9

Thereafter, all three of us would be installed like deities in a row. Carrying small and large spoons, a cup of milk, and a platter of fruit, Rama would seat himself in front of that strange group of gods, all of whom were eager to establish their respective greatness, and he would embark on the ritual of worshiping his young deities. But he was most definitely an astute and resourceful priest. Drawing on his incredible persuasive powers, Rama would make a compelling plea and would somehow manage to convince the young deities to keep their eyes shut while waiting eagerly for some imaginary crow to feed portions of the divine offering to them. As soon as we would shut our eyes, a grape would find itself in someone's mouth, a biscuit between someone's teeth, and a spoonful of milk between someone's lips. Our not peeking, of course, was more pretense than reality, since all of us would continuously watch with half-open eyes the sommersaults made by Rama's dark, thick fingers. And the truth indeed is that I was mortally afraid of the fictional crow's black, harsh, and unfamiliar beak. If with the help of partially open eyes I had not been able to discern that the imaginary crow and his beak were none other than Rama's hands and fingers, I would surely have run away from the scene, forsaking my greed for the holy eatables.

Rama's penance did not come to an end with the conclusion of the breakfast ceremony. He was also responsible for ensuring that no soapsuds would flow into our eyes while we bathed, and at the same time, that our ears would not turn into dry islands. While dressing us, he had to manage somehow to inject an uncontroversial color sense in the haphazard appearance of our clothes; when feeding us, he had to ensure that no imbalance or excess occurred between the quantity of food and the intake capacity of the consumer; at playtime, he had to fill the gap in our world of play by taking on the various roles of elephant, horse, flying cradle, and so forth; and at bedtime, spreading his winglike hands across us while narrating stories, he had the solemn responsibility of transporting us to the gateway of dreamland.

As bottomless as was Rama's affection for us, our high-handedness toward him was equally boundless. One day when we insisted on being taken to the carnival to mark the festival of Dushehra, Rama managed to get permission to take us there only after considerable pleading with Mother. To shop for toys, he seated one of us atop his shoulder and carried another on his lap; getting me then to catch hold of his finger, he said repeatedly, "Do not let go of my finger, Regal One." Even as I nodded my head in agreement, I had already resolved to let go of his finger and set out on my own to see the fair. After wandering around, barely avoiding being trampled upon, it was only when I felt hungry that I naturally thought of Rama. Finding myself in front of a sweets shop, hiding my anxiety as best I could, I inquired of the owner, "Have you seen Rama? He is lost." His dim eyes overflowing with affectionate concern, the elderly gentleman asked, "What is your Rama like?" Biting my lip, I said smugly, "He is very nice." Knowing perhaps how impossible it was to recognize Rama with that description, the old man began to urge me to rest for a while at his shop. I did not wish to concede defeat, but my feet had tired and the platters attractively decorated with sweeets were no less inviting. So, striking a posture of an honored guest, I settled down on a mat in one corner of the shop. Accepting the "offerings" of sweets from the old man, I proceeded to relate to him the story of my grand escapade.

Meanwhile, as he searched frantically for me, Rama's heart was in his mouth. When, after considerable difficulty and numerous inquiries of one and all, Rama appeared toward evening at the sweets shop, I said, filled with triumphant pride, "Even though you are so grown up, you managed to get lost, Rama!" On Rama's wilted face, tears rolled down like dewdrops. Turning me around several times over, he began to scrutinize me as though one of my limbs had been lost somewhere in the fair. When we returned home, I understood that, in the dictionary of adults, such an adventure is known as a crime. But accepting the entire blame for my crime, Rama graciously took all the chiding. What is more, as he put us to sleep, his affectionate pats that night were targeted especially for me.

Once, to clarify for us children the fine, subtle difference between one's own and someone else's possessions, Rama took on the role of a learned preacher. Well, all hell broke loose then! Thus challenged, our brains became active as we fretted over how best we could violate Rama's code of ethics by appropriating something that fit the description of belonging to someone else. That would certainly shock Rama, causing his tiny eyes to fill to the brim with surprise and disappointment.

Our house was joined to a certain Mr. Thakur's house in such a way that it was possible to go from the roof of one house to that of the other. Admittedly, the path connecting the two was merely a foot-wide parapet from which, if the foot were to slip, it would be easy to go directly to hell.

Resolving that the flowers growing in the courtyard of that house would meet the definition of "someone else's possessions," and with the sole intention of vexing Rama, we proceeded to travel that celestial path to steal some flowers. If any one of us had slipped, this story would have taken another turn, but fortunately, we were able to reach the other roof safely. On the last step of the staircase leading to the house below, a bitch was seated along with her small pups. The instant we saw the pups, we were forced to change our original choice of coveted property. As soon as we picked up a pup, at that very moment finding her motherhood challenged, that apathetic canine began to bring the house down by loudly asserting her inviolable right to the pup. Hearing the ruckus, the owner of the house emerged from the living room, somewhat preoccupied in his thoughts, and the otherwise lazy mistress of the house came running from the bedroom. Thus, we found ourselves in a dilemma. What one should do at such a juncture was never featured in Rama's lecture. Therefore, relying on our own good sense, we decided to come clean. We said, "We have come across the roof to steal some flowers." The owner began to laugh. He asked, "Why don't you?" The response from us was even more serious, "Now we would like to steal the pup."

On the way back, we took the more appropriate route. But by the time we reached our house, carrying the pup with us, Rama had come to know of our burglary. Finding that a venomous fruit had grown from his ethical teachings, which he had imagined would serve as an eternal life-giving tree, he must have felt very shaken. Catching the chief of those sky robbers by both ears and flinging that chief high up into what seemed like the space between heaven and earth, he asked, "Tell me, answer me, where were you?" To cry with a whimper had always seemed very disgraceful to me. So, biting my lip with my teeth, I endured that unprecedented punishment. But later, with much controlled anger, I said to Mother, "By pulling my ears, Rama has made them crooked as well as big. Now you must send for the doctor to come and set them right and lock Rama up in a dark cell." She, of course, was oblivious to our crime: Rama, as long as there was life in him, was not capable of squealing. Thus, he had to listen to a lengthy psychological discourse of how not to ill-treat children. He was truly very ashamed of his conduct. But the more he tried to make up with me, the more his royal friend would be reminded of the pain caused to her ears. Even so, in the evening, looking at Rama sitting outside in a dejected state, I did make an offer of truce by asking him to sing a song. Rama knew just one spiritual song, *"Aiso Siya Raghubir Bharoso,"* a ballad about the Hindu epic hero Rama and his wife, Sita. And the way in wich he sang it was enough to scare even the birds and crows from the trees. But we were that unique singer's uncritical audience. Rama used to sing only to us, and we used to listen only for his sake.

My childhood was somewhat different from that of other girls of my age. That is why Rama was especially important. At that time daughters were not welcome. Whenever someone was expecting to give birth, women singers would gather in the courtyard, the kettledrum players assembled at the gate, and, from the elders of the family to the children, all would lie in wait for the birth of a son. The moment that the arrival of the Goddess Lakshmi in the form of a daughter was announced in a subdued voice, a wretched despair would pervade the house from one end to the other. The elder ladies would silently gesture to the women singers to leave, and the elder men would quietly bid farewell to the soundless drummers. If it was beyond the capability of a family to bear the burden of such a guest, there were fairly easy means to return her, like a postage-due letter, back to her sender.

Whether or when such a thing occurred in our clan is unknown. But when, for a very long time, no female child arrived, it then began to cause some worry. Just as the religious custom of horse sacrifice in ancient times could not be performed without a horse, similarly, in the absence of a daughter, it was not deemed possible to execute the noble religious task of giving a daughter away in marriage.

Finally, after much waiting, I was born, and Father understood it to be a special act of kindness from our family deity, Goddess Durga. To express his gratitude, setting aside his great love of the Farsi language, he came up with an epic name: Mahadevi, or Supreme Goddess. Faced with its pomposity, no one would dare give me a short or even a long nickname. It goes without saying that to make me deserving of the name, everyone pumped me with such wisdom and learning from early childhood that my innocent mind began to rebel. Without the illiterate Rama's affection, it is doubtful whether I would have become acquainted with the simple essence of life. As far as I could tell, my instruction had been completed because I had mastered the alphabet. Pointing to the letter *A*, I was able to recall various words beginning with that letter and use them appropriately in conveying whatever was required. In such a context, I must have seemed no less knowledgeable and venerable to my siblings than the legendary sage Shukracharya. After all, I alone had the capability to turn to the books for both affirmation and denigration of whatever feats my siblings were engaged in. And because of that particular talent, they had to be constantly vigilant. Seeing my little brother jump up and down, I would quickly turn to the appropriate page in my book and read aloud: "Here comes the monkey to show his dance!" My little sister could barely turn away in anger when I would recite: "Who cares to console the sulky one; she'll come running when she's done!" Those poor things: they were extremely vexed by my epic knowledge, and they had no means of finding an analogy to any of my acts. But the literate Shukracharya used to get licked by the illiterate Rama. So massive was Rama's treasure of stories, tales, and proverbs that it would not have fit into a hundred books. Accordingly, when my epic knowledge would become the cause of a major conflict, Rama would assume a judge's role, whisper his ruling in everyone's ears, and immediately make peace.

Rama was not opposed in any way to Punditji, who had been hired as my core teacher. But when Maulavi Saheb emerged to teach me the Urdu language, along with a music master and a painting instructor, Rama's heart was filled with remorse. Perhaps he knew that it would not be possible for me to bear the burden of so much accomplishment.

I had begun to fear Maulavi Saheb so much that one day, to escape studying, I felt compelled to hide inside a basket. Unfortunately, that hamper also had a couple of mangoes remaining from the ones Father had sent earlier. As Rama carried the hamper over to where Mother was seated, intending to remove those and replace them with others, he was surprised at its unusual weight. When he laid it down in front of Mother, the situation became most awkward. The moment he lifted the lid, it did not occur to me to do anything other than run. Finally, Rama's and Mother's joint efforts did get me off the hook, and I was excused from having to learn Urdu.

I had no complaints whatsoever against the drawing master because he did not stop anyone from fooling around. Thus, on all the drawing sheets I used to make Rama's portrait by sketching two straight lines and placing a circle on top. When someone else's portrait had to be drawn, I would merely inject some embellishments into that same basic skeleton.

Neither Rama nor I was pleased with Narayan Maharaj, the music master. On the first day of lessons, when he asked if I had any prior training in singing, I informed him with supreme confidence that I was being tutored by Rama. When he requested me to sing something, I sang Rama's familiar spiritual song with such an odd, fractured tone that it left him stunned. Even after that grandiose performance, when he refused to acknowledge Rama as the better and more accomplished singer of the two, it was only natural that he should earn my displeasure.

That the world could function at all without Rama was not acceptable to us. When Mother would plan to take us for ten or fifteen days to visit with her mother, Rama was required to stay at home to look after Father. Without Rama, we were not willing to leave at all. Finally, she would have to leave us behind as well.

When it came to illness, it was difficult to find a more dedicated and caring person than Rama. Once, when my younger brother came down with chicken pox, Rama took the rest of us to stay in the upper part of the house and looked after us so well that we did not so much as remember our brother. Because of Rama's care alone, I did not contract either smallpox or chicken pox.

Another time it was also because of Rama that I was saved from a terrible affliction. The city of Indore, at the outskirts of which we used to live, was experiencing an epidemic of plague. Mother and my younger brother, who was then barely a few months old, were in such poor health that Father found little time to look after the remaining three of us. At such times, Rama would shower us with so much affection that it was impossible to experience any sense of loss arising from Mother's or Father's absence.

Seated on the swing that used to hang from the branch of the thick mango tree, we would listen intently to Rama's unique tales. Around that time, along with fever, I was afflicted by a tumor that appeared close to my ear. Earlier Rama had told us the story of an old woman from whose swollen feet God had made it possible for a brave frog to emerge. Giving Rama the news about my tumor, I said, "It seems that the frog from your story will erupt from my ear." Poor soul, he was absolutely stunned! Afterward, taking a hot piece of brick and wrapping it in a wet cloth, he fomented the swollen area around my ear for a long time, exactly how long it is difficult to say. While he fomented, I cannot recall precisely what he babbled, but I could occasionally discern references to various female and male Hindu gods, such as Devi and Hanuman. For two whole days and nights he did not move at all from my bedside. On the third day, my tumor subsided. But Rama had a high fever. He had developed a tumor, which had to be operated on, and he was very sick. However, Rama was content that I had been spared all that pain. When Mother was able to take us to the feeble Rama's bedside and he beheld us, his dry lips were filled with laughter, his sunken eyes began to swim with enthusiasm, and his weakened body became charged with energy. Mother said, "You saved her life, Rama! Had we not succeeded in saving yours, we would have been left with lifelong regret." In response, after touching Mother's feet with his long-nailed hand, Rama began to wipe the tears from his own eyes. When Rama became well, Mother would often say to him, "Rama, you should settle down now so that you can experience the pleasure of having children." But Rama would always protest vehemently, "No way! What would I do with some wretched offspring of my own! God grant long life and prosperity to these little princes and princesses. They alone will be my salvation." Rama would refer so frequently to his potential offspring that we not only had become acquainted with their fictional state but had begun to think of them as our adversaries. It was somewhat reassuring, therefore, for us to realize that if his children had been like us, he would never have referred to them with such epithets as "damned," "snuffed-out," or "scorched-mouth."

Yet one day, taking out his shoes and other belongings from his cabin and wearing his pink turban, Rama came and stood in the courtyard. Naturally we all felt overawed because we had never seen him so dressed up. Casting a suspicious glance at his stick, I finally asked, "Are you going to beat up those fiendish children, Rama?" Swinging the stick around, he replied laughingly, "Yes, Royal One, I'll give those ruffians such a whack. . . ." But Rama went away, and it is now hard to recall how many days he was gone. All I remember is that in his absence we had to invent new schemes daily to protect our skins from the cruel hands of Kallu's mother, who was stepping in for Rama.

After what may have been merely a short while but to us seemed like eternity, Rama came back one morning, fancily groomed in a pink loincloth and a saffron colored turban. He stood at our door and began to shout, "Royal One, Royal One!" Helter-skelter, we all ran out, but once in the court-yard, we found ourselves awestruck and unable to advance. Rama was not alone! Wearing a red sari that she had tucked up to her knees, red bridal bangles on her arms, anklets round her legs, and with her face hidden behind a veil, the woman standing behind Rama left us feeling at once curious as well as suspicious.

Seeing Rama, my younger sister excitedly started to climb all over him, grabbing him by his shirt. But peeping through the veil that was touching the tip of her nose, a pair of stern eyes began to silently express their disapproval of her action. When my little brother began to insist on being seated atop Rama's shoulder, a movement indicative of a negative nod was detectable from the head hidden behind the veil. And leaning forward when I wished to take a look at that new face, that statue moved away, turning its back to me. How could we possibly be happy with such a stranger? As time passed, the seeds of discord took root in Rama's dark cabin, and the probability increased that the world of our play would dry up.

19

For the cities of our toys to become inhabitable, Rama had served as both the architect and the builder. But now he did not find spare time to attend to his great responsibilities. He would barely arrive and the veiled woman would follow on his heels, and because of her silent hostility, not only we and Rama, but even the dolls, would begin to suffocate. Thus, one day we convened a war committee. Kings are expected to sit on a pedestal. Consequently, I sat on the high table dangling my feet, which were unable to reach the ground; the honorable minister took his place on the chair; and the commander-in-chief settled down on the stool. Then the king inquired in a worried tone, "Why has Rama brought her along?" Shaking his head, the minister repeated seriously, "Why has Rama brought her along?" And covering up as well as he could his inability to enunciate correctly, the commander-in-chief asked angrily, "Tluly [truly], why has she been blought [brought]?"

Afterward, it was unanimously decided by that unique committee that the person who had come to challenge our absolute power deserved to be punished in the name of justice. This task was formally entrusted to the commander-in-chief.

On occasions when Rama's wife was cooking, my little brother would stealthily go and leave some half-eaten cookies in the kitchen, causing the cooked food to be polluted. When she was bathing, he would, with the help of a stick, make her dry sari fall down and get soiled. In this way, she began to encounter countless punishments. But from her there was neither an appeal for mercy nor a proposal for truce. She became even more stubborn in her opposition and began to avenge our wrongs on poor Rama. On her tawny face the impenetrable mask of harshness was always present, and the shadow of anger would never leave her black pupils. Consequently, Rama, who was innocent like us, first became nonplussed, later started to feel helpless, and finally rebelled. Probably he was unable to comprehend how he could place all this time and affection at the disposal of that woman, and if he were to do that, how would he survive? Eventually one day, in anger, Rama's bride left for her mother's home.

It seemed then as though Rama had been freed from some unpleasant bondage. Once again, becoming the ever-happy creator of our unique world, he forgot his wife as though, like a line drawn on water, she had never existed. But Mother found any form of injustice intolerable. She felt that for Rama to discard his wife like our old toys was most improper. That is why Rama began to receive pointed, elaborate sermons on the subject of duty. When he agreed to leave, the same helplessness was evident in his departure as is found in the student who feels compelled to go to the teacher to receive a beating only to honor his father's wish.

When Rama left, it was not possible for him to return. After many days we learned that while he was at his house he had fallen sick. Mother sent him money and wrote to him asking him to come back, but he was meant to travel with us along the path of life only that far.

Arranging our toys before us, we would continue to stare outside with vacant looks. My little brother would wish to cross the seven seas, but the journey was necessarily postponed in the absence of the flying cradle. My little sister was anxious to go for a world tour in her small train, but without the one who could show her the green and red signal flags, it was impossible for the train to go or stop. I was expected to marry off my doll, but without the priest and the caterer, the auspicious wedding date had to be continually deferred.

My youngest brother, who had taken our numerical strength to four, had turned two and a half years old and was becoming adept, day by day, in practicing the destruction of whatever we created. Seating him amidst the toys, after each of us had narrated Rama's story, we all would warn him that when Rama returned, wearing his pink turban and carring his stick, then he would not be able to do any more mischief. But to provide an epilogue to our story: Rama never came back.

Today I have become so grown up that my stubborn insistence that I be addressed as "Regal One" seems like a dream; the tales and stories of childhood seem imaginary; and the charm of the world of toys has become mythical. But even today Rama is true, beautiful, and indelible. Rooted in my past, Rama's gigantic shadow continues to grow alongside the present—silent, watchful, but brimming with affection.

*3 July 1920*

# Chapter 2

Even after the passage of so many years, cutting through the ever-thickening haze that engulfs the past, I am able to clearly recall that pitiful, soft face. Memories of those facial features have merely dimmed with the flow of time; they have not vanished. She had an overly large forehead for her small, round face, edged by two dark, rough strands of hair. Her heavy eyelids, with their long eyelashes, seemed to be making an effort to capture both childhood and adulthood within them. Shaded by the eyelashes were the tearful eyes; her pointed nose was tiny even in comparison to the small face; and her lips were slightly parted, as though taken aback by the laughter imprinted upon them.

Covered with a web of filthy lines from having to take care of all the household chores—clean and dirty, simple and complex—her palms, which were smooth in some parts and rough in others, gave the impression that they were trying to hide their remaining pinkness. Her thin fingers looked somewhat thicker with their lusterless nails covered in black filth. Her feeble, emaciated, but fair arms seemed unable to support the weight of her hands. With its heavy girth, the Marwari peasant skirt seemed to wear down her tiny feet, but her pointed toes suggested a natural delicacy. A streak of dirt, mud-red in color, had been picked up from the courtyard and was sticking to her heels; it looked like the lacquer paint with which married women decorate their feet. How can such memories possibly be forgotten? Countless times in my child-hood, those hands had groomed my tangled hair with so much tenderness. On many occasions, forgetting their required restraint, her feet had moved swiftly to cover the distance from one end of the courtyard to another to open the door for me. It is now difficult to explain how my naive eight-year-old mind was able to connect with her as bhabhi—that is, sister-in-law—particularly since I had never known even a distant, let alone a close, relative who could qualify for that title. Many of my classmates did have very nice sisters-in-law; perhaps their repeated references to them led my mind to create the void that was then filled by that widowed daughter-in-law of a Marwari family.

I still remember that Christian missionary school where the monotonous childhood routine of prayers and study made me so weepy that every day after coming home, until sleep knocked me out, I spent most of my time thinking up an excuse not to go to school the next morning. Those days the chief object of my envy was the maid's daughter: required to cook and wash the utensils, she was at least able to stay at home. I was in a strange dilemma, unable to decide whether the cruel god who had prescribed daily school-going as my particular fate was Mother's own Thakurji or the mission sister's Jesus. If he is one of Mother's deities, I thought, the moment he finds me ducking prayers, he will fly into a rage and further reduce the number of hours I can spend at home. On the other hand, if he is in school and catches me making excuses to stay away from it, he will drastically increase the number of study hours. Unable to resolve the dilemma, I kept wavering between prayers, religious hymns, and other modes of worship in search of redemption.

Yet in that darkness, there was one ray of light. Since the

24

school was nearby, Kallu's aged mother used to walk me to and fro, carting my books. In the course of trooping back and forth, the monotony of school-going was continually eased by the dogs engaged in street fights or by their puppies gone astray. Other happy distractions came from a cat who, seated in a corner, would start to wash her mouth with her paws; or a parrot perched inside a cage on the veranda of some house, mimicking human voices; or hordes of ducks and partridges that would suddenly appear; or the street performers who would show up, along with their male monkeys donning caps, the female monkey wrapped in a veil, and occasionally, even a dancing bear.

Located near our big house was a small structure that served as a shop cum residence. The shop looked glamorous with its stocks of clothing—white and colored, silk and cotton—and its sprkling brass utensils. I never really got to see the elderly Sethji who owned and managed the shop. But my mind was bursting with curiosity about the owner of the eyes that used to peer out at me from the hole in the old canvas curtain hanging on the rear door of that house. Sometimes it would occur to me that I should peek behind the curtain, but Kallu's mother was no less forbidding than the monster who is routinely called upon by the elders to petrify children. Disobeying her could mean anything from having her accidentally hurt my recently pierced ears while giving me a bath to having my hair pulled too tightly while she braided it to getting my tight-necked frock stuck around my eyes while she put it on me. Furthermore, both at home and in school, she was in a position to make many true or false complaints against me. In essence, she had plenty of means to take revenge.

But although Kallu's mother did not like the idea of introducing me to the owner of those eyes, she derived great pleasure in filling me in on that young woman's story. That is how I discovered that she was both an orphan and a victim of grave personal tragedy. Although everyone had told him not to, old Sethji had married his only son to her, and that same year, without experiencing any illness, the son passed away. Soon Sethji became fed up with having to look after his flighty, frivolous daughter-in-law. Understandably, she was not allowed to go anywhere, nor were any visitors permitted. Only on the moonless and full-moon days, some Brahman woman would come, but she was sent away directly after being given whatever was set out as charity—and that, too, happened in Sethji's presence. Sethji, the poor soul, had lost face in his community because of this girl. And yet she was totally shameless! Her father-in-law would scarcely have departed for the shop before she became glued to the curtain. There was absolutely no one in the house to guard over her. She had a sister-in-law who visited now and then, mainly because her own in-laws happened to live in this same town. And on those occasions, the young girl was whipped soundly, without any provocation whatsoever. Kallu's mother would pass on to me all sorts of grim details like these. Drawing on her special vocabulary and with her peculiar gestures and expressions, she would gossip the entire way until we had reached the school. But at that time, those bits of information had about as much significance for me as the story of Princess Bela narrated by my grandmother. The only disturbing realism was that in the present story the princess's eyes continually stared, through the hole in the drape, at the girl who was the listener. Such a situation can hardly be considered satisfactory or acceptable. If all the kings, queens, princes, princesses, demons, giants, and other fairy tale characters were to begin to look at the listeners in this fashion, then the pleasure of listening to stories would soon disappear. That realization

26

came to me while listening to the story Kallu's mother told and while those eyes peeped at me through the hole in the curtain.

As though embedded in that brown canvas, those black eyes would have remained the subject of my imagination but for the events that happened one day. That day, because of the rain, Kallu's mother was held up and did not show up at school. As soon as it stopped raining, I began to walk home alone, and coincidentally, right in front of that curtain, my foot slipped on the wet road. Children usually cry after falling, not because they are injured but because they are embarrassed. Probably that itself must have been the reason for my crying because I do not really recall any injury.

I am unable to say exactly when the owner of those eyes, emerging from behind the curtain, dragged me into the courtyard; but suddenly, out of astonishment, I stopped crying. Looking up, I found a thin but delicate female, more girl than woman, wiping the slushy water from my hands and clothes with the edge of her sari. And from inside the courtyard, I heard old Sethji exclaim with some degree of surprise, "Oh, this must be Mr. Varma's little one!"

From that day on, that house became a source of attraction for me, despite the fact that it had neither a peephole nor a ventilator, not one servant, and no resident guests—not even a pet animal or bird! In that house, which had the appearance of a grave, that adolescent girl seemed like a flower surrounded by an iron parapet: without any companion or mate, denied any sort of merriment or recreation, she was immersed in the perpetual task of becoming an old woman.

The old man used to eat only one meal a day, and she, being a widow, was expected to be entirely indifferent to the business of eating. For her, merely having two meals in one day was proof enough that, tiring of the abstinence that should customarily dictate a widow's life, her mind was straying in some opposite direction.

What was evident, even to my young mind, was how much work she had to do with a body that had become lean from going for such long periods without food and from eating so frugally. Yet sometimes it amused me to see how, sitting on her haunches, she would sweep the massive courtyard and the house, which seemed like the ruins of a monument; at other times, in between drawing water from the well in the courtyard for her father-in-law's and her own bath, she would rest to recover her breath; or, since no washerman had been engaged, she would wash the dirty clothes after pounding them with a small wooden mallet. On the other hand, it would sadden my heart greatly to hear her frequent coughing spasms, which resulted from the suffocating smoke in the cell-like kitchen that remained dark even during daytime, lit only by the glow of the burning firewood. The clanking sound of the utensils as they slipped through her feeble fingers would dampen my spirits further as I would recall how hard she had worked to clean them, burnishing them with a mixture of dry and wet ash and drying them with a cloth to the point where they shone like gold and silver.

But however arduous the work, and however weary the body, I never saw a change in her facial expression, which was always lit by a hint of laughter—nor did I witness any interruption in her routine. That poor soul! Even after doing all that work, her never-ending workday seemed to compete in its endless length with the legendary robe of the epic Princess Draupadi.* Early in the morning, only after spending

*Draupadi was the common wife of the five Pandava princes whose story constitutes the famous Hindu epic known as Mahabharata. At one point in the story, Draupadi is about to be disrobed in public by the enemy when she prays to Lord Krishna to come to her rescue. He does so by extending the length of her *chir*, or robe, which prevents her from being disgraced or raped.

some time bathing and praying to the basil tree,* she would enter her dark kitchen. But by ten o'clock, having finished feeding her father-in-law, she would be free to send me an invitation through the canvas curtain to visit her in the evening. Then she would finish cooking, cleaning the utensils, and pounding and grinding the spices and grains. For the next three to four hours, she still had to occupy herself somehow. Forbidden to step out toward the shop, she would spend her leisure time glued to the canvas curtain, from which only the rear of some houses and one or two passersby could be seen. However, that bit itself was sufficient to spread rumors of her frivolity.

Today I am able to understand fully the pitiable plight of that nineteen-year-old girl whose life's golden dreams, like a dollhouse made of paper or clay, not only were washed away in the flood of misfortune but left her so desolate that it was not possible for her to recall even the shape of her dreams.

In that situation, deprived of any companion, she showered all her desolate heart's affection on me—then merely an eight-year-old child. But since the child was incapable of entering her world, she came to adopt the world of dolls as her own. The old man, too, was so happy to find such an innocent mate for his daughter-in-law that he himself began to fetch and escort me back and forth, treating me with much regard.

As far as Mother was concerned, after merely hearing the story of that orphaned, widowed child, she would turn her face away and cry. But I had no difficulty connecting with her as a playmate, which is how, slowly, my dwarfsized doll, along with her husband, whose head was greatly disproportionate to his body; her lame mother-in-law; a sister-in-law who was unable to sit; and two children who, except for their

*Basil, or *tulsi*, is commonly worshiped as a sacred plant among Hindus.

hands, were disfigured in all respects—all of them, one by one—managed to find their way into my companion Bhabhi's cabin. Not only the dolls but their entire households, from the grinding mill to their ornaments, along with all their means of transportation—from the palanquin to the train—began to inhabit those ruins.

I had seen Bhabhi wear only a white veil and a black peasant skirt or a black veil and a brownish peasant skirt with some white embroidery. In contrast, for every festival very beautiful colored clothes were specially tailored for Bhabhi's sister-in-law. Utilizing some of the fabric scraps that she had collected over time and others that had been brought from my house, Bhabhi would make very skillful provisions to cover my dolls and guard their modesty. Bhabhi knew how to sew her own clothes, such as her peasant skirt and petticoat. As a result, my doll was dressed and groomed like a Marwari woman. In school I, too, had learned to sew *pajamas*, or loose pants, and at home, the *kalidaar kurta*, or pleated shirt. Dressed in these, the male doll looked like a regular business-man or trader. Cutting a hole through a square piece of cloth and slipping it over the necks of the infant dolls, we managed to make them look like the progeny of some primitive age.

Bhabhi was completely illiterate, and thus, my scholarship easily impressed her. By telling her the English names of practically all the animals, and by tunefully reciting a poem in English from the picture book, I struck her dumbfounded. By reading aloud from the Hindi book stories such as "Moth-er's Heart," and "Brother's Love," I brought tears to her eyes. And by telling her of my having written to my mother's brother, I awakened in her mind the memory of her father's sister living in some village near the town of Bikaner. Often she would sigh and say, "I don't know the address, otherwise I would mail her a letter after getting you to write it."

The most difficult time would be when old Sethji's married daughter would come over. After she left, there would be large, black burn marks on Bhabhi's feeble, fair hands and blue marks still visible on her feet. But the moment she was questioned about them, she would divert my attention to some doll-related problem.

Around that time, having recently learned embroidery in school, I embroidered big blue flowers on my light green sari. Bhabhi adored colored clothes. Consequently, when she saw that sari, she became charmed and mesmerized almost as though she were seeing a beautiful painting.

I am unable to comprehend even today why I persuaded Mother to buy me the exact same material to serve as a veil, and why, without letting anyone know, I began to embroider blue flowers on it.

That poor soul! She would send for me repeatedly, even tempt me with new clothes for the dolls. But unable to persuade me to stay longer, she would walk me to the door looking most dejected and sad.

Then one day, hiding that veil so that no one could see me carrying it, I quietly went to surprise Bhabhi. What transpired then seems to have been inscribed in my memory with molten iron. It must have been Sawan Teej, the festive day celebrating the rainy season, since I recall that in place of the drab and dull school uniform, I had been asked to wear a striped sari with a gold border. And in the morning, rather than ordering me to sit down and study, Mother had even applied henna to my hands.

Sitting in the courtyard with her back to the door, Bhabhi was sifting something when I walked stealthily to where she was seated, unfolded the embroidered veil, and put it around her head. Startled, she got up hastily. To begin with, she was crazy about colors. Added to that was the realization that, setting aside my dolls and toys, all by myself and with my own tiny hands, I had embroidered a veil of such massive dimensions for her. Not surprisingly, for a brief moment, she completely lost sight of the fact that colored clothing was forbidden to widows. Like a little girl delighting in a new toy, almost in a trance, she wrapped the veil around herself and, hugging me gently, she began to giggle.

Suddenly, hearing someone calling out to her in a stunned voice—"Daughter-in-law!"—she came out of the trance and found her shocked father-in-law steadying himself against the door. Meanwhile, her eyes burning with anger like embers and appearing as sharp as a naked sword, the sister-in-law had already crossed the threshold. Most certainly it was the festive day of Teej, since the old man had himself gone to bring his daughter over to his house.

Thereafter, what transpired is too tragic to recall. I have never since witnessed such a display of cruelty. Perhaps it was because I saw no way to protect her that I began to howl loudly. But her redemption came only after she had fallen unconscious.

Exactly how the old man escorted me home, and for how many days afterward I lay in fever—all those details are hidden behind a dense fog. But what is clear is that after many days, when I saw her again, in her childlike carefree eyes the darkness of gloom had already settled. Her lips, in which earlier a smile used to be hidden, would tremble now as though weary from the effort to hold back her sobs. That single episode had aged the little girl, had turned the young lady into an old woman.

Sometime afterward, we left the city of Indore, and only after the passage of several years was I able to enquire after her. When I did, I learned that in place of the small shop, a huge skyscraper had been constructed, which had been around already for several years. I also came to know that long since, entrusting the burden of his daughter-in-law's care to the world, the old man had died. However, I do not know to this day exactly how the harsh world looked after her. Although I can well imagine the plight of that small bubble floating in the massive ocean of humans, even so, sometimes I can't help wishing that I could meet her once more who in my childhood had overlooked her own life's desolation to inhabit my dolls' household and decorate the world of my toys!

Even today when someone expresses curiosity and questions me about my aversion to colored clothes, the past comes to haunt the present. How can anyone understand that whenever I see colored clothes, an utterly tragic and withered face slowly begins to crystallize? Reflected, at times, in all the pitiful, weary faces that arise before me, Bhabhi's face links me to itself in an unbreakable bond.

Often I wonder . . . after the old man shut his eyes never to open them again, what had become of the woman to whom he had denied even the right to look at the world? And then, fearing some undefined sinister outcome and responding to some unspoken question, gathering all the affection I am capable of feeling, my heart starts to weep in agony—No! . . . Never!

*11 October 1933*

# Chapter 3

I cast a glance at the thin, young girl with frightened eyes who seemed withdrawn, as though she had willed herself to be an introvert. Then, returning the completed admission form to the gentleman seated in front of me, I said, "You have not filled in her age correctly. Please do so, or there will be a problem later."

"No, there is no error. She turned fourteen last July."

Taken aback, I looked closely at my prospective student, who seemed to be bereft of the playfulness of a nine-year-old and not yet acquainted with the shy demeanor of a fourteen-year-old. My curiosity about her mother must have become apparent; without my asking, the man said, haltingly, "She is my second wife, and as you know, a stepmother is not . . ."

Barely listening to the rest of what he had to say, I found myself mentally traveling across time through the gallery of memories and encountering there the faded picture of Binda, or Vindhyeshwari, buried beneath the passage of what seemed like two aeons. I caught myself saying quietly in my mind, "I know; surely I know."

Binda was my childhood friend from that time when I had not yet grasped the unerasable difference between life and death. Aware that both my maternal grandfather and paternal grandmother had passed away and were in heaven, I had already assured my entire family, in full earnestness, that when I was tall enough so that my head touched the top of the clothes cabinet, I would certainly visit heaven to look them up. No one felt it necessary to oppose this noble plan, nor did I comprehend the rule that once dead, there is no coming back. In such a state, how could my mind even imagine, let alone accept, a mother dying and forsaking her small, helpless children? Naturally, my worldly experience then was somewhat limited. The companion of my childhood, a white bitch, used to guard her pups so fiercely as they rested with their eyes closed in a dark enclosure beneath the staircase that her snarls were enough to dampen even my affection for her. The brown cat, too, grabbing her micelike, helpless kittens by her razor-sharp teeth, would carry them to and fro with such gentleness that not a single tooth would scratch them. On countless occasions I had observed kernels and insects being carefully fed into hungry little beaks that emerged from the pigeon's nest in the terrace corner and from the sparrow's nest behind the huge painting. Likewise, when weaning her calf, the anxiety of the black cow, which was conveyed to the entire household through anguished bellows, was also apparent to me. And clearly, the beggar woman who went from door to door—with one child glued to her shoulder and another clasping her finger—was, after all, seeking alms only for her children. Thus, I had understood in a conclusive way that the world's entire business is centered around feeding and nurturing children and that the task of ensuring that this noble duty is performed without error has been assigned to the category of humans designated as "mother."

Binda also had a mother, whom we used to call Punditayin Chachi, or Punditayin Aunty, and Binda addressed her as Nayi Ma—that is, New Mother. With her fair, fat body draped in a colored sari, she would sit on the cane bed and rub oil on Mohan, the little one, whose eyes sparkled like blue glass buttons above his puffy cheeks and flattened nose. Her well-fashioned hair, which was sprinkled with red sindoor powder, was indicative of her married status and looked like a thick line of red ink. I found all of her adornments—her sleepy eyes covered with black, threadlike eyeliner; her shiny earrings and necklace; her gem-studded, multicolored bangles; and her toe rings with bells—extremely pleasing because they made her look doll-like.

Outwardly, she appeared fine, but her conduct was somewhat unusual. At my house we were pampered on winter mornings, usually awakening only after the sun had come out. After being given a hot bath, we would be dressed warmly in socks, shoes, and woolen clothes and then gently urged to sip lukewarm milk. Conversely, in the neighboring house, Punditayin Aunty's voice would be escalating from shrill to shrillest. If that raving and ranting had been altogether incomprehensible, I might have equated it to our black cow's bellows and assumed it was a display of maternal affection. However, since I was somewhat familiar with Aunty's vocabulary, I could not possibly be confused. Even my innocent mind would sense the stream of harshness that flowed from comments such as, "Will you get up, or do I need to come and fetch you?" and "Why do you stare with your buffalo-like bulging eyes?" and "When will Mohan's milk be warmed and ready?" and most sad of all, "Cursed soul, even death does not come to you!"

Occasionally, I would climb to the terrace to try to understand better the intricate web of relationships in that family, and then I would spot Binda, draped in a soiled, coarse sari, spinning like a top from the courtyard to the kitchen. Sometimes when sweeping the floor, and other times when lighting the stove, fetching water from the courtyard faucet, or serving a cup of milk to her New Mother, Binda appeared

37

to me like a magician, since I considered the completion of so many chores to be humanly impossible. But when I heard Aunty's harsh resounding voice oblivious to my surprisingly open curiosity—occasionally interspersed with an admonition from Punditji, her husband—an unknown sadness would cast its shadow around me. Even after considerable thought, I was unable to comprehend what wickedness the well-behaved Binda—whose conduct was paraded before me as exemplary, to keep me from being naughty—was quietly up to in her home. I, myself, never had to do any chores, and indeed, I created havoc day and night—yet my mother never cursed me, wished me dead, or threatened to gouge out my eyes. Once I even asked my mother, "Is Punditayin Aunty not like you?" How much mother understood of what was implied in my question, I do not know. But her brief response of "Yes" was able neither to solve Binda's problem nor to resolve my confusion.

Binda must have been somewhat older than I, but looking at her shortness, I felt as if someone had pressed her down from above, making her even shorter. Moulded with thin skin like the membrane that covers the frame of the two-bit timbrel drum, Binda's hands and feet, through which her greenish veins were visible, appeared to be paralyzed by some unknown fear. At the slightest sound from anywhere, she would startle easily, and her entire body would quiver at the very sound of Aunty's voice. Her unusual reflexes not only added to my sense of bewilderment but also made me fearful. And Binda's eyes reminded me of a caged bird.

Once when gazing up at stars, counting them one by one, Binda pointed to an especially bright star and said, "That is my mother." Then, of course, my astonishment was bound-less. Does everyone have one mother residing in the stars and another in the house? When questioned, Binda offered a few particles of wisdom from her treasure of knowledge, and I understood then that the mother who is called away by God turns into a star and continues to keep an eye on her children from above, and the one who comes all dolled up to live in the house is like Binda's New Mother. Since I do not know how to accept defeat easily, after some reflection I said, "Why don't you address your New Mother as 'Old Mother'? Then she won't be new any longer, and she won't need to scold you." Binda did not find my solution suitable, since she had clearly seen her old mother carried out of the house in an open palanquin and the New Mother brought in a closed palanquin. Thus, it was difficult for her to agree to alter either woman's designation.

My mind was truly troubled with Binda's story, and that night I said to my mother with a true note of urgency, "Don't every become a star, no matter how radiant a star God offers to make of you." Poor Mother, surprised as she was at my unusual request, was barely able to speak when I bluntly explained what I meant: "Otherwise, a new mother like Punditayin Aunty will come to our house in a palanquin and put an end to our milk, biscuits, *jalebis* [doughnuts] and other treats. And I will have to be like Binda." I do not recall Mother's reply, but I do remember that on that particular night, I was able to fall asleep only after clutching the edge of her sari in my fist.

Though Binda's crimes were unknown to me, I became fully acquainted with the forms of punishment meted out by Punditayin Aunty's court of justice. In the hot summer afternoon, I had seen Binda stand for hours on the scalding surface of the courtyard, repeatedly lifting her feet and setting them down. I had found her tied daylong to the kitchen pillar, her face wilted with hunger, and had observed her fanning for hours the New Mother and Mohan, asleep in the cradle. She had to bear punishment not only for the offenses she committed but also for those she did not. The thick, black, curly hair detected in Punditji's dinner plate was obviously Aunty's, yet it was Binda who was punished. Though tangled, starved of hair oil, and incapable of being washed by her small hands, I always liked Binda's hair because of its natural tan color and its softness. When Punditayin Aunty took the scissors to Binda's hair, scattering the clippings across the garbage heap, leaving merely a few strands of hair to cover her scalp like the black stripes on a cat, I found myself close to tears. Binda, however, remained seated and still, as if both her head and hair belonged to her New Mother.

Another day from Binda's sad life comes to mind. On this day, when the milk on their stove was coming to a boil, Binda's small hands managed to take the pot off the stove, but then it slipped from her fingers and fell. Standing at the door, I was dumbstruck to see Binda crying; her feet were burned from the scalding milk. It was difficult enough for me to comprehend why she could not ask Punditayin Aunty for medication to treat her burns. On top of that, when Binda, placing my hand on her loud beating heart, urged me to hide her somewhere, her situation became a total mystery to me.

I took her to my house, of course, but was able neither to take her upstairs to my mother nor to find a safe hiding place. Punditayin Aunty's sharp, petrifying voice vibrated through the walls, confounding our sense of direction. In sheer confusion, we went into the room where the cow's fodder was stored. Once inside, I found myself being poked by sharp blades of straw and troubled by the darkness inside the cell. But clasping my hand between her cold hands, Binda continued to sit quietly, hiding her charred feet beneath the prickly hay stack, which appeared to have transformed into a silken bed.

I suppose I had gone to sleep soon afterward. Only when Gopi came to collect fodder—and upon discovering the two of us, started to create an uproar—do I recall waking up, rubbing my eyes, and asking, "Is it morning already?"

After applying some sesame seed oil and limestone water to soothe Binda's feet, Mother sent her home with a special messenger. What Binda had to face after returning to her place is hard to know for sure; evidently, in Punditayin Aunty's code of justice, there was no place for pardon, no right of appeal.

For several days I did not see Binda working in the house or the courtyard. Mother had stopped me from going over to her house, but often she would go there herself, carrying grapes and apples. After much cajoling, Rukiya revealed that a Maharani* (empress) had come to visit that house. When I asked, "Can I not meet her?" the amused Rukiya had to stuff cloth in her mouth to stop laughing. Neither convinced nor consoled by what Rukiya had said, I sneaked over to Binda's house one afternoon to see things for myself. In the deserted, lower part of the house, Binda lay on a bed alone. There were dark circles beneath her eyes; her pox-filled face looked like nothing I had known; and her body, hidden beneath a dirty sheet, seemed inseparable from the bed. It was inconceivable to me that one could be so ill yet see nothing of doctors, bottles of medicine, a mother gently patting one's head, or a father nervously pacing around the bed. So I stood there next to that isolated Binda, who had no one there to fuss over her, and I felt so stunned I could only stare vacantly. It was Binda, in fact, who explained to me, through some gestures and incoherent words, that the New Mother, along with Mohan, was living in the upper section of the house, possibly because

*A common euphemism for smallpox in India.

of fear of contracting smallpox. Morning and evening, some woman came to do Binda's work.

After that, it was impossible for me to see Binda again; because I had disobeyed her command, Mother became more worried and much stricter. One day very early in the morning while mother was praying, I don't know what Rukiya said that made her so quickly close the Holy Scripture, *Ramayana*. Drying her tears repeatedly, she proceeded to Binda's house. On her way out, she instructed me not to leave the house. Consequently, I felt compelled to peek into Binda's house from wherever I could so as to discover the truth for myself. For me, Rukiya was no less than omniscient, but without considerable entreaty she would not reveal anything, and to supplicate her was against my self-respect. Peeping from the window, I could see little else but a crowd of people gathered at the door. I was used to seeing crowds converging for a marriage and for the arrival of the bridegroom's party, so I wondered, "Is a marriage taking place in that house, and if so then whose?" Such questions began to test my wisdom. Punditji's marriage could occur only after the second Pundit-ayin Aunty died and turned into a star, and it was impossible that Mohan, who was yet unable to sit on his own, would be getting married. Mulling this over, I came to the conclusion that Binda's marriage was taking place, and she had not even invited me! Injured at this unthinkable insult, and with all my dolls serving as witnesses, I proceeded to vow never to invite Binda to any auspicious event.

After peeping into Binda's house for several days, I finally asked my mother about Binda's expected return from her in-laws. Only then did I learn that she had gone to be with her mother who resided in the sky. From that day on, I often looked for Binda amidst the smaller stars scattered around the big shiny star. But from such distance, was it possible to recognize her?

Since then much time has passed, but I am still unable to close the chapter on Binda and her New Mother. Whether that will ever be possible, who can say?

*5 August 1934*

# Chapter 4

As a name, Sabiya is an abbreviation of neither Shabnam nor Shabrat. It is, in fact, a derivative of the Hindu Savitri, the mythological heroine whose piousness and unflinching devotion to her husband enabled her to convince Yama, the Lord of Death, to bring her husband back to life. To be honest, it is hard to say whether it was really our benevolent Aryan tradition that was merciful enough to allow this lowest of the low-caste Harijan to gain respectability through the use of this name. More likely, Sabiya's parents, who could conventionally be said to have departed to heaven but were actually hell-bound, stole this name like a clever pickpocket. And later, to claim it as their own, they chopped and modified the name so much that it is now difficult for anyone to establish an exclusive claim to it.

As if to defy my rule never to fire or change servants, my old sweeper, without seeking my permission, proceeded on that grand journey from which it is impossible to recall anyone. Only then did Sabiya appear. Holding a ball of flesh wrapped in a dirty rag that could perhaps qualify as a month-old infant, she materialized one day; with her other hand she led her five-year-old daughter, whose nakedness was covered only by her filth. Sabiya's face appeared to be moulded from oily, black clay, but in every line there was the same structural grace and harmony as one often finds in statues made out of plaster of paris. Round rather then elliptical, her eyes had the frightened, puzzled look of a child lost at a crowded fair. Around her hands and feet the thick bracelets and anklets crafted from dull, lusterless nickel made her look like a chained prisoner. Decorating her narrow forehead, above her linked eyebrows, was a small, round disc made of yellow-colored glass, suggestive of the yellow flower blooming on the furze shrub over a rubbish heap. Draped in a faded sari that must have once been red in color but now resembled the shade of a rusty water pot, Sabiya looked like a statue laboriously carved out of clay by an amateur sculptor: although all its ephemeral color had faded, bonded to the statue's graceful contours, the clay beneath was still visible.

I learned that Sabiya's husband had simply taken off without her knowledge. At that time she was confined to the lying-in chamber, having just given birth. Shattered at her husband's departure, she fell sick and was replaced in the bungalow where she worked by another sweeper. She told me that if I could give her a job, she would then be able to raise her children. Ignoring her assurance that she would put body and soul into serving me, I cast a suspicious glance at the tiny bundle and asked, "How are you going to be able to work dragging this infant along?" Patting her filthy, skinny daughter's back, Sabiya shook her head confidently. When she began to elaborate on her daughter's uncommon skill in looking after her baby brother, giving actual examples, I was able neither to laugh nor to stop myself from smiling. Frankly, having observed the darkness that spread across little Bachiya's glowworm-like eyes, it seemed brutal to burst out laughing and uncharitable to keep mum.

After explaining what work was expected of her, I had barely made it back to my room from the veranda when, crashing through the barrier of awe in which she held me, my

old maid Bhaktin's curiosity erupted into countless questions.
Bhaktin was an untiring gossip: to know everything about
everyone was the principal aim in her life. It seemed as though
God, who is Himself the supreme storyteller, had blessed
Bhaktin's tongue with the narrating talent of the legendary
Yojnabahu. From the thousands of questions strung together
like a rosary for Sabiya, some scattered words forced their way
to me. And the touching quality of the responses alone made
it impossible for me to be indifferent to them.

I was really not able to hear clearly the question that
Bhaktin asked Sabiya about her husband, but from the response—"No, ma'am, he couldn't have done anything unto-
ward; he was, after all, a married man"—it was clear that
Sabiya was close to tears. In response to Bhaktin's "That
woman must have cast quite a spell!" Sabiya said defensively
and in a feeble voice, "Ma'am, it's all one's fate." I tried then
with considerable effort to concentrate on my writing, and at
that point I lost track of the rest of Sabiya's story. By and by,
I learned that not only was Sabiya's husband in no way an
approximation of the noble Satyavan, the legendary Savitri's
husband, but worse, he had been unable to live up to even the
meaninglessness of his obscure name, Maiku. Evidently, one
day, without giving any inkling of where he was headed, he
ran off with someone else's new bride. That was shocking
enough, considering that the bridegroom was someone from
his own community and more like a caste brother. To make
matters worse, Maiku left just when Sabiya was tending a
three-day-old baby. From then on, she gave up all hope of his
ever returning, and there was no further news of him. Partly
to avenge himself and partly out of a desire to rehabilitate his
deserted household, the spurned bridegroom invited Sabiya to
move in with him, but she turned him down. Finally,
recognizing the wisdom of the old saying, "One who has been

scalded by hot milk blows on even buttermilk, waiting for it to cool down," that wretched fellow opted to marry his elderly, widowed sister-in-law and breathed a sigh of relief.

In view of what had happened, it is hardly surprising that everyone began to refer to Sabiya as an eccentric, although personally I was unable to detect any trace of eccentricity in her other than her mania for work. Every morning at the crack of dawn, spreading a torn, soiled cloth on the rocky ground under the margosa tree, she would lay down her infant. Partly to look after the baby and partly to wave away the flies, she would leave Bachiya to sit with him. Tying her waist tightly with a tattered rag, she would grab the broom. Then, on one end of the yard, accompanied by the swishing sound of the broom, Sabiya's dance would commence. She seemed to simply float through the air! And at the other end of the yard, Bachiya would begin her antics. Sometimes adopting an austere posture and at other times a heroic one, Bachiya would shoo away the flies with her tiny hands. Adding to her theatrics, she would skip on one foot or jump on both feet to scare away the crows. Bachiya's mother had a slender body that was agile like a green twig rather than rigidly inflexible like a dry stick, which indicated life instead of lifelessness. In contrast, the sapless body of the girl showed not the agility of a new leaf but the helpless movement of the soft petals of a closed bud that is covered with frost and unable to blossom—a state more indicative of inertia than of growth.

The area beneath the margosa tree outside my window was Bachiya's stage, and important spectators, such as my dog and the hostel's cat, were certainly welcome there. But there was also nothing wanting in the hospitality extended to stranger crows, unknown birds, and squirrels living in the margosa tree. Yet judging from Bachiya's keen vigilance, it appeared as though everyone, from the dog to the birds and from the squirrel to the flies, was eager to kidnap and abscond with her darling brother. To scare off those disguised bandits, she would resort to speaking in a variety of languages—ranging from a cat's meow to a bird's chirp to heaven knows what else. At the end of it all, she would blow through a kazoo whistle that could have cost no more than a nickel, as though she were announcing a truce by sounding a conch shell.

Piercing through the fortress of her dedication to duty, when pangs of hunger would rattle her insides, Bachiya would open the knotted edge of that same dirty rag on which the baby was resting, and taking out a small piece of bread, she would come to terms with the hidden enemy. But admittedly it was impossible to carry out that task in the presence of so many spectators. Once, imitating a rooster, she tried to scare a crow away, but the insurgent crow snatched her only weapon against hunger and flew away with it. Finally, by sending her some cookies and a corn-flour doughnut, I was able to perform the noble task of replacing a wooden dagger with a machine gun in her battle against hunger. From then on Bachiya used the sound "cock-a-doodle-do" to call me to her rescue; whatever foodstuffs I sent in response carried traces of grudging acrimony from my maid Bhaktin, who did not relish the thought of being asked to wait on Bachiya.

By ten o'clock, having finished all of her tasks, Sabiya would fold up her act like a conjurer and go for her bath. By the time she returned to pick up her food with her shiny, brass plate she had scrubbed to a sparkle, the leisurely dining activity in the hostel would be over. I had given strict instructions that the leftovers from the plates in the hostel's canteen should be fed to the bullocks plying the school's carts instead of being dumped on sweepers or other low-caste people. My unconventional command that Sabiya be served fresh rice and lentils from the kitchen rather than the leftovers

49

most certainly caused enough resentment among both the cook and the dishwasher to add a caustic flavor to what was dished out to Sabiya. Of course, Sabiya herself was too hesitant to complain about anyone, fearing that by doing so, her mouth would become covered with burning blisters.

Seeing that she was burdened by her children and that she carried her food platter twice a day, both morning and night, with great difficulty, I suggested that she feed herself and her children in the compound itself. Her reticent response seemed more like a confession of guilt to some major, unpardonable offense: "Bachiya has an aged, blind granny, Ma'am. Without first feeding her, how can I eat?" After that it was pointless to say anything. But I could not help feeling angry at Maiku for casting the burden of his blind mother, along with two small children, on Sabiya. Men are incredible. For their pettiest of comforts, they do not think twice about causing some woman terrible grief, and they do it with such impunity as though simply giving the woman her due. Moreover, they are willing to take on an obligation only when it seems as pleasant and palatable as sugar-coated quinine. The moment they sense unpleasantness, their first inclination is to leave everything and run.

Sabiya's inexplicable generosity had understandably caused me to feel such affection for her that she spent her time well under my protective care. Then one day, acting as an interpreter for Sabiya, who stood hidden behind the screen door, Bhaktin said that Sabiya required a "nice-ish" sari. I gave her permission to give away the coarse hand-spun cotton sari that was hanging on the clothesline to dry. But Bhaktin made a grimace and said. "Nicer!" So I began to search my wardrobe for a sari that would qualify for that vague epithet.

From the days when I still wore silk, a blueish silk sari, whose color had faded from repeated washing, fell into my hands. Casting that in front of Bhaktin, I tried to concentrate on my work. I never wish to know more than what someone willingly tells me, so I did not probe this untimely demand for a sari. Bhaktin, however, insisted upon making up for that deficiency in my nature. She was a source of amazement, not only to others but to me as well. No matter how pressing my work, she would seat herself somewhere within earshot and continue to narrate, for my benefit, the entire world's saga on the pretext that she was really talking to herself. Although I reprimanded her for this countless times, her conduct did not change. Having left behind her orchard of eighteen mango and five mahua trees, a mud house, and several acres of farmland; and having broken her ties with her three daughters, her sons-in-law, and her grandchildren, Bhaktin never considered the possibility of leaving and going back to her village from the moment she joined me. Even if I withheld her wages, she would not leave. Likewise, if I denied her food, she would make do with some parched grain and molasses from the village. It seemed that she would leave me only to go to heaven, and even then unwillingly. Could one ever reform such a stubborn person? So despite my reprimands, Bhaktin continued to play the role of Sanjay, who narrated the events of the epic war of Mahabharata to the reigning king Dhritarashtra. The difference was that Mahabharata's Sanjay relayed the news of the war to the blind Dhritarashtra after having been specifically requested to do so, in order to give him the benefit of his sight. But to avoid listening to Bhaktin's unsolicited stories, I often had to feign deafness.

Ah, yes! So I gathered from Bhaktin that Sabiya's husband, Maiku, did come back, but not alone. Along with him came Gainda, his new wife, for whom he made arrangements to stay as a guest with some sweeper employed at the train station. Poor Sabiya, she went out of her mind with joy! That very day she ran around trying to organize a religious gathering to express her gratitude to Lord Satyanarayan. Even after such a reception, Maiku maintained a long face. After considerable probing, he told Sabiya about Gainda and implored her to let Gainda live with them. And as if that were not enough, looking at Sabiya's silk sari, he said entreatingly, "This doesn't really do much for your dark complexion, Sabiya. Give it to Gainda; it will look terrific on her."

Without uttering a word in protest, Sabiya took off the blue sari and gave it to Maiku; donning an old sari, she went to fetch Gainda, ignoring her blind mother-in-law's attempts to stop her. But one could see that she was heartbroken. While working in the yard she would often rest her head against the margosa tree and sob; and at other times, she would pause in her sweeping to wipe her eyes. Poor woman! How long had she waited for Maiku! And how much she would miss him! But when he returned it was with Gainda. On top of that, it never occurred to him to ask Sabiya whether she was happy or sad, nor had he asked about the children. On the contrary, putting all his trust in Gainda, he was easily led to believe her backbiting and false allegations against Sabiya and was ever-ready to pick a fight. And Sabiya's burden increased even more, since Maiku had not yet found work.

One day, having dressed the wheat-complexioned, round-faced, insolent, and lively Gainda in my blue silk sari, Sabiya brought her to meet me. In the conventional manner of seeking blessings from elders, Sabiya said, "The younger one touches your feet, Ma'am." Great! What blessing could I give her? "Be happy" would imply that she should continue to cause Sabiya pain. So I said, "God give you wisdom so that you can live in harmony."

Barely four or five days later, Sabiya presented herself again. She was in need of five months' advance wages, which, at the rate of ten rupees per month, amounted to fifty rupees (around two dollars). Surprised at her request, I asked her why she needed the advance. It came out that Gainda's former husband and other caste brothers were creating a fuss. Only if the caste elders, who were to serve as arbiters, were fed a fitting meal would they have the energy to cope with the burden of mediating this grave dispute. Because of the unusually civil manner in which Gainda's former husband had behaved toward Maiku and Gainda, there was little doubt that he would need a fitting compensation for the damage caused to him and to his reputation. Not compensating him for his excessively cultured behavior would certainly amount to slighting the very concept of self-sacrifice. However, even after recognizing the indisputable logic of the situation, I could not watch Sabiya starve her children to pay for that noble but costly act of compensating the victim. So I shelled out part of the amount she had requested. When I later learned that, to arrange for the balance, Sabiya had sold her necklace of gold coins, which was her late mother's parting legacy, I felt great remorse. I should have known that having accepted a responsibility, that woman was incapable of not carrying it out.

Even after the caste elders granted Gainda permission to move in with Maiku and Sabiya, the latter's hardship did not lessen, because Gainda would quarrel with her incessantly. Nevertheless, when I would see Sabiya at mealtime carrying lentils in a big, metal pot and *roti* (bread) and rice on her plate, my mind would be filled with wonder. After being charred with so many burning embers, her generous heart was still capable of giving refuge to others. Just as she did not fret over her young children's mischief, so she did not pay heed to her husband's heartless ungratefulness or to her co-wife's inappropriate sarcasms or to her mother-in-law's groundless reprimands. To her it was as if they were all her children, and their shirking of their responsibilities did not make her oblivious to her own obligations toward them. Sabiya's response to anyone who mentioned Maiku's unworthiness or criticized his conduct always took the form of a simple, brief question: If Maiku had gone crazy or were inflicted with some dreaded disease, what would everyone have advised her to do then? No matter how illogical her response, it certainly spoke to Sabiya's goodheartedness. She obviously did not fall into the category of women who are guillible enough to allow a house, car, or wealth provided by a husband to make up for his wantonness. Neither could she be counted among those God-fearing, penance-driven women whose virtue is guarded by stern religious canons that serve as fierce and vigilant watchmen. Nor could she be included among the submissive, frightened women over whose wavering heads society's naked sword is forever dangling. Falling outside all those categories, she could only be described as the most wretched of human beings. How then could one explain the presence of this precious touchstone in the person of Sabiya, whose mere touch could turn the surface of any sort of iron into gold?

In all those years, only once did I find Sabiya despondent. That day Maiku and Gainda had gone to a fair in some village and had not yet returned. In their absence a theft occurred in a neighboring bungalow. In such a situation, it is well known that persons of high status, who themselves have become wealthy with the money plundered from others, hand over to the beastly police not only their servants and other staff but also the poor from the neighborhood. Although it is unlikely that they can recover even a penny of the amount stolen, in their insane rage they do not rest until they have shredded the remnants of dignity from the lives of the poor. Frightened to death at the thought of being caught as a suspect, Sabiya stood before me, saying, "Now I don't know whether we can be saved," and quietly started to cry; her anguish touched my heart in a unique way. The value society has placed on female honor alone is no measure of her greatness. Inside her being is inscribed another measure that is loftier and more indelible. That is how a woman who trades her flesh, with the full knowledge and backing of the entire world, can still find that she is able to keep her chastity alive in her heart. On the other hand, bound by society's structures, the chaste woman who makes an occupation out of virtue can still devote herself, with every breath, to creating an unchaste woman.

Finally, somehow, the crisis that had overtaken Sabiya blew over. How that happened is not really relevant to her story.

Pointing to the honorable and diligent Sabiya, the wife of a lawyer associate once said to me, "Why do you hire the wives of thieves as your servants?" When I heard that remark, my cool demeanor became like the raging water that has the flow and force to cut through soil and stone. Quite unexpectedly, I found myself saying, "If appropriating someone else's wealth by some means or the other is considered a theft, I want to know which wealthy woman among us would not be called a thief's wife?" The dark shadow of shame that spread across the face of the person who had asked the question undoubtedly caused me anguish; but it was clear that the arrow I had shot had pierced its intended target.

In essence, it is true that I find Sabiya approximating that powerful womanhood in our mythology that succeeded in push-ing life's frontier from this to another, unknown world. If that legendary woman, Savitri, was compelled to fight death for life, then this one, Sabiya, was battling with life in order not to die.

*3 March 1935*

# Chapter 5

Kulmani had not yet returned from the bazaar, and as I sat waiting for him on the rock beside the edge of the lake, I began to feel bored. From focusing my eyes on the oscillating reflection of the leaf-fringed branches in the water, my vision had become strained as I tried also to practice controlled breathing or pranayam. Suddenly, upon hearing "Oh, this must be Mahadevi!" I turned to face the nearby road. Striking an unusual acrobatic posture, almost as though she were balancing her obese body on two thin high heels, my old friend became visible.

My relationship with that mountainous region has been very close, like that of a child to a foster mother, and in recent years that terrain indeed seems to have become my mother. Traveling on foot across several hundred miles, I have seen its tranquil beauty and superior life in countless forms. But I have failed to resolve fairly the competing claims of the mountain's still beauty and the city's clamor. Leaving the lap of my dust-filled home in the plains, I seem to find comfort only at the snow-white feet of the mountains, which devotedly absorb the pollution while preserving their compassion for us safely inside their gigantic, fortress-like forms.

I have never liked the idea of transplanting the cyclonic life-style of the plains to mountainous regions. I have always felt that hill resorts, such as Nainital and Mussoorie, which are embellished with all the trappings of modern city life, are like unskilled actors who lose their identities to assume another's role but are unable to perform it successfully. When my doctors, concerned with my fever, advised me to reside in the hills for a few months, it was only after considerable persistence that I was able to get their permission to live three miles away from the clamor of Nainital, in a place called Takula. But once a week it was necessary to consult with the doctor, and while my servant, Kulmani, purchased the necessities, I would wait for him on the somewhat desolate left bank of the lake.

That particular day, however, I was truly delighted to run into my childhood friend. I had no reason to find an excuse not to visit her in the bungalow where she was staying with her two small children. Who can deny that, after the passage of time, when two friends meet again they try in so many ways to relive their lives? So placing before each other the sketches of our lives, we spent some time comparing our experiences.

Adding spice to our otherwise dull memories of the past, my friend told me that a gentleman whom we both knew had brought his third, newly wedded wife to Nainital for sightseeing. The enormous astonishment in my eyes could not translate itself into words. The old man must have seen at least fifty-four springs and autumns. It was indeed as if his two earlier wives, unable to keep in step with the swift pace of his life, had chosen to renounce his companionship. Each of the two women had borne him a son; one son did some sort of business in Calcutta and the other had become the "property" of his in-laws, meaning that they totally controlled him. Owning two houses and some other assets, the elderly gentleman felt it necessary to seek out another mate in hopes of making his retirement more colorful.

Compelled by my silent curiosity, my friend spoke in a somewhat reassuring voice, "Have no qualms. This time he has emancipated someone who is thirty-five years of age and has been a widow since childhood." Hearing me exclaim "Impossible!" my friend began to smile, matching the measure of my disbelief with her derision. After some debate, she decided to introduce me to this third wife on the way back.

The old man was staying with his wife in two rooms above a shop in Mallital. Hearing us knock at the door near the staircase, the woman, who meekly invited us to come in after apologizing for her husband's absence, seemed extremely spiritless, emaciated, and sickly. A new gold chain appeared to mock her neck, which was constricted by thin, sapless, protruding bones and was covered with the parchment of wrinkled, blood-drained skin. A pair of earrings fabricated in a somewhat archaic style seemed ironic next to her spotted, withered face and flattened cheeks. Her eyes were big, but on that wilted face, beneath her uneven eyelashes, they seemed as if they had been superimposed, and that with one blink, they might be ejected. Her lower two teeth had been broken, probably due to a fall, as one was entirely invisible, and the other, only half visible.

This spiritless, weary woman, who, after crossing the long span of more than three decades of widowhood, had agreed to be the wife of an old man with one foot in the grave, filled me with wonder. That shrunken statue wrapped in a faded, silk sari had neither form nor health nor traces of rapture or ambition. Then why had she decided to settle down again? That question began to haunt my mind.

If that first meeting had turned out to be the last, there would be nothing left to say today. But it so happened that soon after descending the staircase, we ran into the old man, who was carrying some apricots tied in his handkerchief, and he welcomed us effusively. With every breath he invited us to get better acquainted with his new wife, and thus I came to know the misfortunes of that strange "fortunate woman."

Being the only sister of three brothers, she was brought up with much affection. Her marriage occurred when she was young enough to be totally innocent of its implications, and widowhood, too, arrived without her understanding. Just as the first situation had not caused her to float in merriment, the second did not cause her to drown in despair. The death of their son within a year of his marriage had caused her in-laws not only to repudiate her but to believe that even uttering her name would bring a curse upon them! Her own anguished parents did not deem it appropriate to stand by and watch their daughter become a charred victim of the angry blaze of her in-laws' wrath. After all, they had raised her caringly, as though she were a fragile doll. To make that unfortunate blow on her somewhat bearable, her parents showered all their affection on her, allowing her to want for nothing. And thus, the child-widow began to lead a sheltered, self-contained life, like the princess of some fairy kingdom, cursed but unaware of the basis for the curse.

Even when her mother passed away, because of the presence of her father there was no change in her status. But the moment her father closed his eyes for good, it was truly as if everything in the world around her had changed. With the destruction of that sole shield, innumerable blows rained upon her, and since she could not divine their source, she had no idea how to defend herself. Thus far, her late husband had seemed to her like God, who, although removed from our senses, remains the basis of our firm faith and unwavering belief. Like a thoughtful devotee, without reasoning, she had lived her life in blind devotion.

Thus, when the wives of her brothers first began to blame

her for her husband's death, or when neighbors started pointing to some vague shortcoming and rained sarcasm on her,
she felt deeply bewildered and hurt. Her heart in fact felt a
jolt like that experienced by someone suddenly awakened by a
spark from burning embers. Those around her found new
ways every day to torment her mentally and physically. For
starters, the household staff was reduced. So it was at first by
allusion, later explicitly, and finally in a commanding tone
that she was ordered by her brothers' wives to take over all the
work. She was also admonished by them for routine oversights. To make matters worse, the sisters-in-law, who had
once doted upon her every wish, began to claim that her
brothers must surely be noble souls who had strayed from
Satyuga, the mythical Golden Age—or else, how could they
willingly undertake to feed a parasite? Such a suggestion, of
course, was completely new to her. She did not understand
why she should drown them in a sea of gratitude for being
able to continue to live in the house where she had been born,
and why she should be thankful to her brothers for providing
the food and clothing that she had earned by working hard
day and night. After all, only the elder brother was in a
salaried job; the other two simply looked after the assets that
belonged to the man who was her father as much as theirs.

By and by, in that venomous atmosphere, her body became
feeble and her spirit broken. She began to suffer from chronic
fever and fainting spells. Someone said it was an early symp-
tom of tuberculosis; another suggested it was epilepsy. Both
diseases were then considered contagious; consequently, her
poor sisters-in-law became agitated, fearing for their own and
their family's well-being. After mutual consultation, a letter
was written by her younger brother and dispatched to the
younger brother of her late husband. But from her in-laws
came the grim response that they did not care to recognize

her. They suspected that because of some improper conduct on her part, her brothers were seeking to dump her on innocent people. Should they persist in doing so, the courts of justice were always available for their protection.

Left with no solution, the older brother's wife said to her husband in a voice laced with affection, "Nowadays, of course, widow remarriages do occur. How would it be if we were to marry poor Bitto off?" When the inquisitive brother wondered about his sister's preference in the matter, his wife, commenting in a loving tone on his naiveté, explained that such a desire would not be voiced even by the most immodest of girls. Bitto, of course, was shyness personified. But if marriage did not occur, it was certain that she would slowly suffocate and die.

In a society where a sixty-four-year-old man desires a fourteen-year-old as a wife, it was not easy to resolve the problem of remarrying the thirty-year-old Bitto. It was truly her good fortune that no man who had lived to the ripe age of 150 was found! And it must have been the blessed outcome of her unbroken virtue from previous lives that a fifty-four-year-old fogey took upon himself the responsibility of her deliverance.

At first, when her brothers' wives told her of the happy news of the prospect of a second marriage, it seemed from the vacant look in her big eyes that she could not comprehend such a piece of information. When it finally did register, its effect was exactly contrary to expectation. Bitto opposed the marriage with pitiful lamentation. But neither the seas nor the mountains can block the path of the "benevolent!"

Someone explained to Bitto the necessity for her to look out for the welfare of her brothers and nephews. Another drew her attention to the contagiousness of her disease. And yet another proved to her the uselessness of her infirm, threadbare body.

Probably thinking the old man to be nearing death, no one worried about his welfare. Finally, at an auspicious moment, having saluted the threshold of her father's house for the last time, Bitto passed through grim-looking drapes with burning but tearless eyes and entered the house that had been settled and unsettled several times. Not a soul was present either to welcome her or to protest her arrival.

This same pitiful story, minus an epilogue, Bitto told me in segments over several meetings. It was precisely because of its gravity that her anguish had turned incomprehensible. Given our society's patriarchal structure, it is hard to predict the extent to which a man would be able to fathom her pain adequately. Poor man: his powerful puritanism and singular dedication to accomplishment have been generally ruptured by woman. Thus, he has composed volumes to explain the nature of this supposedly deceitful other sex.

When woman makes a particular commitment and internalizes any truth as her own, man remains neither a subject of importance nor a cause of fear for her. It has never been possible for man to accept this fact. Very likely it is only to convert his defeat into a forced victory that he continues his attempt to consign her to countless unequal settings and to bind her to complex social and religious restrictions. It seems that not only the means of affluence, but even a fistful of flour, command greater worth than the entire life of a woman. Even so, my mind cannot accept that a woman, although bruised by circumstances, is truly beaten as long as the radiant flame of courage still burns in her heart.

Finally, one day I helped Bitto settle her baggage on the bus, and I bade farewell to her. But her story continued to inhabit every corner of my heart. So from time to time I have found it necessary to inquire about her by writing to my friend who originally introduced us.

Today, almost four years later, I have received an unusual bit of news. My friend has written that the old man, afflicted with an intermittent fever, is counting his last breaths. While the daughters-in-law have stayed away, both his sons have come and launched the sacred task of taking possession of the house, his wealth, and other assets. The noble sons cannot stand the sight of their third stepmother, so it seems that poor Bitto's future is now more bleak than ever.

I am tempted to write an elaborate sermon and send it off to my foolish friend warning her that if we do not wish to spend eternity wandering through purgatory because we have challenged the sanctity of sage Manu's ancient sayings about women, we should be prepared to concede that Bitto is definitely harboring the desire for a third marriage somewhere inside a lonely corner of her heart. And in this sacred land, and especially in this enlightened age, there is no dearth of benevolent old men perpetually ready for her deliverance. If this is the case, then where is the need for all this lamentation and fuss over Bitto?

*4 January 1935*

# Chapter 6

Can that golden, pleasantly cool spring evening ever be forgotten? Flapping their stretched wings, the morning's minstrels were returning to their respective nests in rhythmic flight. Guided solely by the sound of their wings, the sun seemed to shoot golden arrows at the birds through the space between the intermittent thin clouds. But their insane speed was throwing the arrows off target.

Just as I turned away from witnessing that festival of colors in the west, my servant came in and told me that an elderly gentleman who had not given his name had been standing outside for a long time in hopes of seeing me. To tell him to come back the following morning would most certainly have fallen on deaf ears, like a cry in the wilderness.

Since I was busy writing and had only composed the first line of my poem, I was somewhat annoyed at the disturbance. What work could possibly be more pressing than my work? I wondered. Whatever his urgency, the visitor's untimely appearance managed to abort my poem like an idol that is shattered even before it has a chance to be consecrated.

With all the pride my heart was capable of mustering, I was about to protest his arrival by saying, "I am a poet!" But better sense prevailed! Being a poet does not excuse one from being civil, I thought. Had not the irony hidden in that realization stung me so deeply, I would not have bothered to get up. Feeling a bit vexed and unsociable, without really noticing what I was doing, I put one foot in a new slipper and the other in an old one and rushed out. But as swiftly as I went out, with the same swiftness I suddenly found myself standing speechless in front of that unwelcome visitor. Sometime during my childhood I had seen an artist's rendering of the legendary sage Kanva; that painting had come alive, as it were, in this old man. He had milky white hair and his face was framed by a white beard, which was suggestive of a threadlike, milk-based sweet; his face was etched with wrinkles, showing clearly the arithmetic of time. At one time perhaps lustrous, his eyes that day seemed dim, like hot air fogging up a shiny mirror. In a split second I sized him up from his white head to his dust-covered feet, taking note also of his somewhat old, black sandals and his hand-spun cotton cap, which had been washed but was now edged with a border of perspiration and dirt. Vaguely I said, "I am not able to place you." His eyes, dimmed from experience but luminous with tears, looked up for just a second; then his eyelids with their petal-like eyelashes lowered, either from the weight of suffering or from shame.

In a weary but grave voice he said, "What could be a better introduction to the person who is standing at your door to seek your help than the fact that he knows your name? My granddaughter is most anxious to meet you just this once. For two days I have been struggling to decide whether I should disturb you. Today I have mustered up enough courage to come: this courage may not last until tomorrow. That is why I was stubborn about meeting you. Would you be willing to take the trouble to come? The carriage is waiting."

I stared at the old man in utter amazement. Both my acquaintances and those who do not know me well are aware that I simply never go anywhere. He is probably a stranger, I thought to myself, so I inquired, "Can't she come here instead?"

I could not understand the basis of the old man's embarrassment at my question. Although his lips moved, no sound emerged. Turning his face away, he tried to hide his moist eyes. Seeing his distress, I asked whether any illness had prevented her from coming. With a completely despondent expression, the old man nodded his head in affirmation. In a few, somewhat scattered words, he explained that his granddaughter had become an orphan at the age of eight and a widow at the age of eleven.

There was not much time then to argue or discuss: the old man's granddaughter must be near death! Poor unfortunate soul! But I am no doctor or practitioner of indigenous medicine, I thought. And while it is customary for people to include poets at head-shaving and ear-piercing ceremonies, they have not yet begun to invite poets to preside over the final moments of a person's life. In such cases, a priest is invariably summoned to recite the Holy Scripture *Gita*. However, the hope with which the old man studied every expression on my face finally forced me to say, "Let's go! Let me take someone along, though, because it will be dark by the time we return."

That day I became acquainted with the town's streets: spread out and mutually entangled like veins in which dirty sewer water flows like tainted blood, and where bare-bodied, filthy children walk around like germs of disease. When we arrived, we somehow managed to climb the steps of a three-storey house and reached the top floor. On the veranda, seated on a soiled, torn mat and resting against a pillar, a statuesque woman became visible. In her lap, wrapped in filthy clothes, was a ball-like shape. Leaving me there, the old man walked across the inner room to the balcony on the other side. As he stood there, his weary form, which was battling his broken heart, began to look like some silent but pathetic scene from a faded film.

As the invitation for me to approach her was delivered in the form of an indifferently spoken "Please come," I looked intently at the woman, probably the old man's sister, beckoning me to come closer. On approaching her, I was truly amazed to see how much she resembled the old man in her appearance: the same build, the same shiny but misty eyes, and the same sort of quivering lips. Through her unkempt hair and filthy clothes, her toughness appeared as pitiful as a sword that had been dug from the ground after having been buried for many days. A somewhat vexed voice said, "It's very kind of you to have come. God alone knows the hardship we have had to endure in the last five months. Finally now, we are free! But just look at this girl's stubbornness! She begins to sob at the very suggestion of giving the child away to the orphanage; if there is talk of leaving it in someone's care, she protests by going on a hunger strike. Repeatedly we have tried to make her understand that it is improper to try to drag into this crisis someone like you with whom she has no prior acquaintance. But does she listen? Hardly! Poor old man! He was most reluctant to go. But after he could not convince her, he had no other option. . . . Now only if you are in a position to rescue us can our lives be redeemed."

Though at first speechless at that elaborate yet pithy background, when I recovered slightly, the situation slowly became apparent, like objects at the bottom of a pool after one has been in the water for a while. I would be lying if I did not concede that my body was trembling, my feet were becoming stiff, and beads of perspiration were forming on my forehead. I have often theorized about social ills, but this was the first time I had encountered such a dreadful, phantom-like vision

68

of life. Targeting my social activism, almost everyone in my family had tried to convince me, shaking their heads in despair, that my noble ideals could not bear the blast of the blazing heat of life's stark, grim realitites. Nurtured in the tender shade of my pious dedication, my dreams, too, would choke in that suffocating smoke. I have responded to these criticisms repeatedly with the same answer: it has never been, nor will it ever be, possible to wash off slime with slush. To wash it off, clean water is needed. I have always believed that it is only the boundless purity of the lotus, which refuses to let even the pearl-like water rest on its petals, that allows it to be rooted in mire.

Finally, standing there and feeling somewhat ashamed of myself, I moved that dusty shawl aside and took a close look at the one who had been the cause of the upheaval. Holding him in her arms was the old man's sister, who seemed to be the image of anger. Her lap emitted nothing but contempt; that, along with the filthy cloth in which the infant was draped, seemed to put a stamp of invisible tragedy on the baby's tender face. The infant's oily, dark, short hair, which was glued to his forehead with perspiration, looked like the black-colored letters of the alphabet. As his eyes were shut, his eyelashes formed two half-circles on his cheeks. Like a small, red bud, his mouth had fallen open in sleep, and there was a strange sort of smile on it, as though he were having a beautiful dream.

He has no idea, I thought, of how many hearts, which had once overflowed with affection, were now dried up because he had been born—or of how many dry eyes that were now flooded, or of how many who now found it difficult to carry on with the process of living. This uninvited, unwanted young guest—what did he know, even about himself? His arrival had not made his mother respectable in anyone's perception. To welcome him, no nuts had been distributed; no songs of merriment had been sung; no grandfathers on either side had thought up countless names; no older and younger aunts had argued over their share of the rewards offered to relatives and servants; and no father had seen in him the image of his soul. Not only that, in the cursed fate of this out-of-wedlock child, providence had not given him even the right to his mother's lap—something to which the child of even the poorest of the poor and the most oppressed of oppressed women is entitled.

Protecting herself from society's cruel scorn, living anonymously in the worst hell, and struggling alone with her affliction, when his mother did finally give birth, it seemed that the mere touch of her breath transformed him from an extinguished charcoal into a burning ember. No one is concerned about how he will survive. The only worry is how, without taking on one's head the burden of murder, one can do the kindness of freeing him from the burden of life! When my mind could no longer endure the weight of that solemn gloom, I got up and expressed a wish to see the young mother. In response, the aunt indifferently pointed a finger to a dim room to the left of the veranda.

As I entered, nothing was clearly visible at first; only the rustling sound of clothes, similar to the sound of a snake slithering, directed my attention to a shadow-like figure. But in a few moments, when my eyes became accustomed to the dark, I picked up the matchstick lying next to the oil lamp on the ledge and lit it.

I do not recall having seen such pitiful tragedy elsewhere. I cannot accurately portray the pitiable figure I encountered or the foul mat that was spread on the cane bed; or the terribly wrinkled filthy sheet, and the pillow covered with oily stains. She did not appear to be more than eighteen years old, but she seemed ever so feeble and helpless. On her dark but blood-drained yellow face, I noticed her dry lips and her eyes that seemed to burn like the flame of an oilless lamp.

Guessing her mental state from her unnatural inertia, I sat down on the high settee next to her pillow after removing the small metal pot resting on it. And then, suddenly, with unknown provocation, the silent grief in my heart transformed into a thousand angry sparks of fire.

For her untimely widowhood, she could not be blamed. That someone deceived her and wrongfully impregnated her—she could not be held responsible for that either. But there was no question that she alone was responsible for the life and death of that child, who was an integral part of her body and soul. Just because a man did not accept her as his wife, should she, because of that falsehood, renounce the one incontrovertible truth of her life—her child? Even if no qualifying adjective exists to characterize her, the fact that she had given birth to a child would still have bestowed upon her the edifying epithet of *Mother*. And now she was trying to renounce her obligation to her child? For what? Just so that she could return to that fraudulent society where, after taking a dip in the holy Ganges, and after fasting, penance, and prayers, she could disguise herself as a chaste widow and have the freedom to commit similar oversights? Or perhaps it was so that, in some home for widows, she could be auctioned off like an animal to the lower or the higher bidder? Or possibly it was to slowly give up her life by swallowing poison, one drop at a time?

Woman is never more vulnerable than when she has her child clinging to her bosom. In no other situation is she so fiercely aggressive, like Goddess Kali, as when she defends her offspring. Perhaps that is why the covetous world, fearing her power of motherhood and seeking to strip her of her maternal armor, leads her inside the chakravyuha, the legendary maze, and, by shooting arrows, makes a sieve out of her. Gathering their out-of-wedlock infants in their arms, if these women were to say daringly, "Barbarians, you have taken away our womanhood, wifehood, and all, but we will not in any way surrender our motherhood!" their problems would then be instantly resolved. A society that refuses to accept and honor women for their courageous, sacrificing act of motherhood is hardly likely to worship them by placing their cowardly and pitiable images on a pedestal. For aeons man has been punishing woman, not for her strength and defiance but for her forbearance.

I had become so agitated with my charged emotions that I cannot accurately recall today what transpired then. But I remember her arising from the cane bed and kneeling down; then encircling my feet with her feeble arms, she hid her face in my knees. And I, sensing her eyes silently shedding tears, felt my heart confounded with remorse.

Interlacing indecipherable words with her silent tears, she tried to explain to me that she was not willing to give up her child. If her grandfather disapproved of her decision, then she would have no recourse but to seek my help. In that case, I would need to make an independent arrangement for her subsistence: nothing more than one bare meal a day. She would be more than happy to wear whatever clothing I discarded, and she had no other expense. And once her child grew up, she would spend her entire life putting her heart and soul into whatever work I chose to assign to her. Furthermore, she asked that, as long as she did not commit another offense, I let her have the same claim over me as she would have been entitled to had she been my daughter. She did not have a mother, which is why she had been reduced to this miserable state. So if I could now shade her with the protective cover of motherly love, she would be able to live safely with her child.

Putting my hand on the head of that child-mother, I began to wish fervently that it were possible to grant her wish. Little did this innocent seeker of my protection realize that in this age of slippery ethics, where morals are shed like autumn leaves, it is easier for a woman to be stoned for deviance than honored for her moral strength. So at twenty-seven years of age, I accepted the charge of an eighteen-year-old daughter and a twenty-two-day-old grandchild.

The old man considered returning to his place of birth, which was not likely to be sympathetic to him in the light of what had happened. It would have meant spending his remaining days mocked by a scornful society and renewing his association with derisive, cruel neighbors. But the feeble claims of those mundane inclinations were buried in the lofty call of duty.

Today that old man is in some unknown world. Like a gust of wind, he dragged me into a thorny forest and deposited two flowers with me, from whom I have received only the fragrance of affection. Yes, one of the two flowers has a complaint that I do not find the leisure to listen to her story, and the other says that I do not narrate to him princely tales.

*21 November 1935*

# Chapter 7

What hidden impulse from the present manages to trigger, in all its vivid detail, some forgotten story from our past? If that question were simple to answer, then I would know why I am able today to suddenly recall the image of that scrawny, timid, young student who, like a tiny wave after touching my life's coast, disappeared into the fathomless sea.

It was only after sensing the inexplicable attraction that I have always felt for the ruins of Jhoonsi across the River Ganga and for its neighboring villages that people started teasing me about my eternal connection with that place. And that connection, indeed, is something to wonder at! Whereas most people safeguard their leisure time for meeting close friends or for participating in festivities and other recreational activities, I spend that time—happily so—on the bank of the River Bhagirathi, whose waters rage at the mauled and injured feet of those ruins.

Over time I have also become acquainted with the women who routinely emerge from their doll-like homes. Located either near or far, some of the houses are painted and white-washed, others dilapidated and old. The women come to fetch water from the river in sparkling brass and copper vessels or in brand-new pots of red clay or even in old pots whose colors are tarnished. Some of the women are dressed in embroidered red saris or in plain white ones; some in saris whose fabric has become one with the grime settled in it; others in somewhat newer saris; and still others in saris so tattered that they have holes like a sieve! In the sticky parting of one woman's hair, the finger-wide red streak of sindur powder glows in the rays of the setting sun, while tiny strands of tangled, dry hair, which have never known the grooming touch of even crude hair oil, surround the face of another, accentuating her dejected look. On the tan, round wrist of one woman, the artificial gems on her bangles, which were bought in the city, sparkle on and off like diamonds. On another woman's thin, dark wrist, dirty, yellow bangles made of lacquer look like thick lines of muddy sandalwood drawn on black stone. Another woman seems to be trying to hide her arms, which are covered with metal bracelets, behind the screen of her water vessel, while another appears bent on flashing her bracelets and anklets, without whose musical resonance she could not walk or talk. From yet another's ear, lacquered loops shaped like pennies flash occasionally through the portion of the sari that covers the hair, while some other's heavy earrings, which are attached to a long chain, appear to link the neck to the cheek as if they were one. On the fair, tattooed feet of one woman, the silver anklets seem like beautiful circles, while the black, tarnished, metal toe-rings and anklets around another woman's wide toes and fair heels remind one of well-scrubbed iron fetters.

They begin by washing their hands and faces, and afterward wade through the river to fill their water vessels. Setting the pots down on the river bank, they then arrange the headgear on which the vessels are to be placed. Occasionally I find some of them looking toward me, their faces breaking into faint, bright, sad, or happy smiles. Perhaps aware of the distance between us, they never forget to bridge the gap with their smiles.

The cowherds' children, too, are aware of my presence as they graze their cattle, quickly chasing the occasional stray cow with a stick. Similarly, upon seeing a goat or a sheep heading in my direction, the shepherds' children quickly grab the truant animal by its ears and drag it back to the herd. Even the boys, who are idlers with nothing to do except waste time playing billi-dunda all day, manage to acknowledge my presence with oblique glances.

Milkmen who go across the river to sell milk in the city, laborers who go to the neighboring fort to work, and boatmen who are busy either launching or anchoring their boats can at times be heard singing a song: *"Chunari ta cangaoub lal magethi ho"* ("Let the veil be dyed red"). But the moment they realize that I am listening, they stop abruptly, out of reticence. From some of them who pride themselves in being more civil, I manage to evoke a shy greeting.

I cannot say exactly when and how it occurred to me to bring a smattering of education to those children. But without appointing an action committee or electing officeholders or having a school building or making an appeal for donations— and essentially without any conventional trappings or cere- mony—when my students assembled around me under the thick shade of the *pipel* (fig) tree, it was only with considerable difficulty that I was able to assume the air of solemnity expected of a guru.

And how can I describe what those seekers of knowledge were really like? With hoops dangling from their ears and bracelets around their wrists, and dressed in clean *kurtas* (shirts) and short *dhotis* (lower-body garments), some of them seemed a quaint mixture of the urban and the rustic. Others wore oversized shirts that might have belonged to their older brothers, since they nearly touched their toes, and reminded me of the scarecrows in the fields. There were others who, because of their protruding veins, enlarged stomachs, and crooked, emaciated legs, could only vaguely approximate the definition of human offspring. And still others appeared to have gathered the entire world's contempt inside their lifeless, dim eyes and in the tender gentleness of their emaciated, pale faces. But Ghisa stood alone amongst them, and today only he comes to mind.

I have never been able to forget that particular dusk. It seemed as though on the reddish-gold flowing garment of the evening night had furtively cast a spell with black eyeliner. My boatman was studying the rough waves with some concern. Having put away my books, papers, and pens, and having loaded them on the boat, Bhaktin, my old maid, was grumbling away at the growing darkness, or perhaps at God for making me slightly crazy. Poor thing! Having spent ten long years with me, she considered herself more a guardian than a servant. But what did she get out of it, except the experience of having to live with the unpleasant consequences of my whimsical nature? Suddenly those thoughts filled my heart with tenderness for her. As I started moving toward the boat, I spotted a female figure walking in my direction through the growing layer of darkness, and I came to a sudden halt. On her dark, somewhat longish face, her thin, blue lips became even more conspicuous. Her narrow eyes were moist with anguish. Her plain, faded, borderless sari made of thick cloth had managed to cover her bare torso. Yet one could easily sense her graceful form. In the fading light, I could not clearly see the emaciated half-bare child clinging to her feet; the woman held him by the shoulder with one of her hands.

From the woman's halting words and gestures, I was able to deduce only that she did not have a husband, that she cleaned other people's homes for a living, and that her child, who was left all alone, just loafed around. If I were to let him join the class with the other children, he would be able to learn something.

The following Sunday I saw him sitting all alone, crouched behind everyone else. Of dark color but graceful in build, he had a scrawny face in which two pale but alert eyes were embedded. The firmness evident in his tightly closed lips and the roughness of his short, ungroomed hair seemed to defy the shy softness of his face. His shoulders appeared somewhat bent from having to support his neck, in which his veins were clearly visible; with filthy, anemic palms and hands with ragged nails, his thin arms loosely swayed from his bent shoulders like two artificial limbs of an actor playing the role of the legendary four-armed Lord Vishnu! In his limp body, only his small feet seemed especially sturdy, probably from his continuous running. Yes, that's exactly how he was: with no touch of poetry either in his name or in his body. However, his alert eyes were filled with some inexplicable curiosity. Routinely, like a clock, those wide-open eyes would fix on me as though their sole aim was to acquire all my knowledge.

Other boys were somewhat withdrawn or distant from him, not because he was of the low, weaver caste, but because someone's mother, another's grandmother, and yet another's aunt had explained to them, after boxing their ears, the absolute necessity of staying away from Ghisa. Indeed, the boys revealed this to me along with the mysterious reason for his coming to be known by that ugliest of names, Ghisa— which means one who is dragged around. Evidently, his father had passed away even before he was born. With no one at home to look after him, his mother would move around with the child glued to her like a monkey's baby. When she would get busy with her work, she would lay him down on one side; later, when he began crawling around on his stomach, the child began to acquire, along with his first experiences of the word, the appropriate credentials for that name.

Gradually, other women, too, while passing by, would stop me, and with all sorts of facial expressions and odd gestures, start to acquaint me with Ghisa's congenital inferiority. Thus, I came to know something other than just his name.

His father was most definitely of the low, weaver caste, but he was extremely proud, and aspired to become a gentleman. Giving up the occupation of basket weaving associated with low status, he managed to learn some carpentry. To make matters worse, by quietly bringing a young bride from another village he managed to slight all the beautiful young women of his caste and disappoint their parents. Man may be capable of bearing such injustice, but at such moments, God's intolerance is well known. Thus, just as he started to live in style from his earnings from building the villagers' doorframes and whitewashing the landlords' houses, God chose cholera as a means to strike him dead. And like all mortals, he had neither the intellect nor the resourcefulness to cook up an acceptable excuse to decline God's invitation to join Him in His abode. His wife, as it turned out, was no less proud than he was. Many of the village's widowed or unmarried weavers, out of sheer generosity, showed eagerness to take on the burden of looking after her. Not only did she give a flat "no" for an answer, but she did so with a bite. Adding insult to injury, she said, "Having been the bride of a tiger, should I now accept moving in with a jackal?" Later, shedding her tears without pomp and ceremony, wearing her hair down, smashing her bangles, and donning a borderless sari, she assumed the role of a widow from an upper-class family, an act that threw the society around her into a sea of turmoil. And to top it off, Ghisa was born after his father passed away. He was born, in fact, six months later. But what can be said with certainty about time, when a single moment sometimes appears like a year, and at other times, a year seems to turn into just a moment? Consequently, if the initial six months got stretched like a rubber band into a year, how could the villagers be faulted for such an exaggeration?

This sad story, which was told to me in several installments, had been narrated with the specific intent of changing my mind about Ghisa. And the change did occur, except that, instead of inclining toward the storyteller, I leaned toward the story's leading characters. In that way, Ghisa became even closer to me. Perhaps he had not been able to fully grasp the slander related to his birth. But the impact of even the little bit he understood muat have been considerable, because he would go around scrupulously sparing everyone from coming into contact with his very shadow, as though he had some contagious disease.

No one was as clever as Ghisa when it came to learning a lesson, grasping it before anyone else, and applying it to his conduct. A conscientious student, he did not allow his book to have even a single stain, he kept his slate sparkling, and he shouldered with great earnestness the responsibility for even the pettiest of tasks. Consequently, I sometimes felt tempted to borrow him from his mother and seek her permission to have him stay with me, allowing me to provide for his further education. But he was the sole support for that slighted but proud widow. I knew for sure that she was not ready to say goodbye to her late husband's place of residence, and I could clearly see how unbearable her life would be without her son. Moreover, judging from the conscientious nine-year-old Ghisa's devotion to me—merely his teacher—I realized the strength of his attachment and commitment to his mother. And that is how Ghisa continued to live there, amidst those very tough circumstances in which the cruelest of fates seemed to have left him merely for its own amusement.

On Saturday, using only his feeble hands, he would cover the shade beneath the pipal tree with an oily, yellow layer of cow dung and clay. Then on Sunday, as soon as his mother left for work, he would stuff under his arm a bundle of ragged cloth containing a thick *roti* (bread), some salt or parched grain, and a small piece of jaggery, and he would once again sweep and dust the shaded spot beneath the tree. Then he would come and squat on the bank of River Ganga where, covering his pale, alert eyes with the shade of his small, dark hand, he would let his sight travel across miles. The moment he got a glimpse of my blue-and-white boat, he would fly like an arrow toward me, and without addressing any of his companions by their names, he would yell "Guru Saheb!" (Respected Teacher) for everyone to hear. After he reached the tree's shade, the final repetition of this routine became once again necessary. My mat, resting on the low branch of the tree, would be taken down and spread on the ground after he had dusted it several times; the inkpot made of brittle glass, black with the stain of dried ink that had never been used, and the grayish-green pen with its tarnished color and broken nib would be taken out from the hollow of the tree and set in their appropriate place. And then the strange superintendent and extraordinary student of that unique school would move forward slightly, ready to welcome me with folded hands.

I was able to go there only four times during the month and sometimes, because of excessive work, I had to skip one or two sessions. But even in that short period of a few days, what I got to know of that child's inner being has remained with me and is ever vivid, like a photo in an album.

Even today I am unable to forget the day when, without making allowances for their clothing, I drove those poor souls to exhaustion, instructing them on the value of hygiene. On the following Sunday, all of them appeared before me as before—only some had managed to wash their faces in the river water in such a way that the grime was now merely streaked. The hands and feet of some of them had been scrubbed so that they appeared as separate attachments to the rest of the bodies, which were still dirty. And still others had left their oil-stained ragged shirts at home, hoping that, by destroying the evidence, they could be free from the suspicion of crime. From their skeletal forms, it seemed as though their heartbeats were proclaiming the astonishing fact that they were alive, although no one would find their death surprising. But that day Ghisa was missing from the crowd. When I inquired about him, the boys began to whisper to each other, and all seemed eager to explain the reason for his absence. Slowly, piece by piece, I managed to put together the fact that Ghisa had been asking his mother for some soap from the moment he heard me rave about hygiene. His mother did not receive her wages, and the shopkeeper did not agree to barter soap for grain. Only the night before had his mother received her payment, and that morning, leaving all other work aside, she went to purchase the soap. Since she had just returned, Ghisa was busy washing his clothes—recalling what Guru Saheb had said earlier, that they should come to class only after they had bathed and put on clean clothes. Anyway, what clothes did that unfortunate soul really have? An old shirt, one of whose sleeves was ripped in half, donated by some charitable lady, and a towel-like, ragged cloth. After bathing and wrapping himself in that torn, wet towel, and donning the half-dry shirt, Ghisa came and stood before me like a criminal; then not only my eyes but every pore of my body became moist. Only at that moment did I understand fully how, in a famous epic tale, the guru, sage Dronacharya, had tested the devotion of his young pupil by requiring him to cut off his thumb. The use of the thumb was crucial to the pupil, who was eager to learn archery. Yet he chopped it off without hesitation as proof of his devotion. The sacrifice I had inadvertently imposed on Ghisa seemed no less demanding.

One day, for some reason even I could not fathom, I took along ten or twelve pounds of *jalebis* (doughnuts) for my students. But partly because of the cleverness of the seller who weighed them, partly on account of the shrewdness of the one who had been sent to buy them, and partly as a consequence of the grabbing and snatching that occurred when the dough-nuts were distributed, each was able to get no more than five. One of them protested, "I received one less." Another reported that so-and-so had taken his. A third wanted one more for his younger brother sleeping at home. The fourth was suddenly reminded of the need to cater to some unspecified claimant. But in that pandemonium, no one could say exactly when Ghisa took off, carrying his share of jalebis. I overheard one little rogue whisper to his friend, "Son-of-a-gun! He's raising a pup. He must surely have gone to give him some." But becoming diffident under my scrutiny, he fell silent. Eventu-ally Ghisa did return, and he was able to account perfectly for all the pieces: wrapping two jalebis in a cheesecloth for his mother, Ghisa had stacked them safely in the roof; one he fed to his orphaned pup; and two he had eaten himself. On being asked, "Do you want more?" he lowered his eyes shyly, moving his lips ever so slightly. It came out that the pup had received less than he had. "If Guru Saheb has any more to spare, let one more be given to the pup," he said.

One particular event that occurred just before the colorful spring festival of Holi is engraved in my memory with such indelible colors that it cannot be easily washed away, even after the passage of so much time. In those days, Hindu-

Muslim enmity was slowly growing, and there was a high
probability that it would soon erupt into a communal outbreak. Ghisa had been sick with fever for two weeks. I used
to send him medicine, but no proper arrangement could be
set up to nurse him. For a couple of days, his mother stayed
home from work to look after him. Later, arranging for a
blind old woman to replace her, she resumed her work.

On Sunday evening, after bidding farewell to the children,
I proceeded to call on Ghisa. But I had barely walked fifty
feet from the pipal tree when, seeing him coming toward me
on wobbly feet, barely able to keep his balance, I became
deeply troubled. He had been unable to get up at all for the
last fifteen days. I suspected he was delirious. His emaciated
body seemed as if it were charged with liquid electricity. His
eyes were even more fiery, and his face seemed like a piece of
iron slowly turning red on a low flame.

But what was even more worrisome than his delirium was
the tale of his daring sagacity. It seemed he had woken up
feeling thirsty, but finding no water nearby and feeling it
wrong to ask Maniyan's blind granny to fetch him some, he
decided to bear his discomfort silently. Just then, returning
from the other bank and speaking to her from the doorway,
Mulloo's uncle informed the blind woman that riots were
taking place in the city, and that was when Ghisa thought of
Guru Saheb. The moment Mulloo's uncle departed, he left
ever so quietly, so that the old woman did not realize he had
gone. By sometimes leaning against a wall and at other times
against a tree, he managed to come running to warn Guru
Saheb. Falling down and catching hold of my feet, he said he
intended to stay there; under no circumstance would he allow
me to leave.

Then the problem facing me grew even more complex.
Most definitely, I needed to cross over and reach the other

bank. At the same time, I felt compelled to explain the reasons for my departure to Ghisa in such a way that his already delicate health situation would not become more grave. But there was no hint of the eternally reticent, polite, and obedient Ghisa in this resolute and obstinate child. Apparently he had witnessed two slain and wounded boatmen on a very similar occasion a year before. His fever-affected brain, adding lasting colors to those earlier gruesome memories, was making my dilemma worse. But in trying to make him understand, I suddenly struck a chord whose sound was novel even for me. As soon as he learned that I had with me in the college hostel many students who came from afar by train, and who were able to visit their mothers only once during the year, and who, finding themselves alone in my absence, would become agitated, Ghisa's obstinate protest quickly dissolved. Once that happened, no one could match Ghisa's ability to rationalize: "Of course, Guru Saheb must go to be with those who are unable to return to their mothers in the evening. If Ghisa were to stop her from going, then God would be angered. After all, it was God, who, seeing Ghisa loiter aimlessly and alone, had sent Guru Saheb to him." Those and countless such arguments burst forth from him. Even today my eyes begin to water, and I feel choked as I remember them. But that day, when I returned after getting him to lie down on his broken bed, I was truly in awe of Ghisa, who had come dragging his feeble body, burning with fever, to save me from disaster.

Ghisa later recovered. And then a daily battle started between him and the hot summer wind, which moved around furiously, carrying bundles of dust and dried leaves. Even as he swept and dusted, the school would be wrapped in ever more dust and hidden beneath a sheet of brown, yellow, and a few green leaves. And the wind would continue to call out to the dried leaves tangled in the skeletal branches of the trees. Resonant with the hot hissing of the wind, the dusty campus beneath the trees would further aggravate the already frustrated child. So I decided to stagger my school hours, staying there from late afternoon through the evening. But that decision had no impact whatsoever on Ghisa. I learned that he continued to sit day-long under the tree, rubbing his sticky eyes and dusting his books repeatedly, as though he were a celibate ascetic from some ancient epoch who had renounced the world to meditate. And it was only to disrupt his meditation that the hot winds blew so hard.

In that way time passed slowly until suddenly one day, it sprang forward, like a child racing to touch the finish line, to that particular day when I was supposed to bid farewell to those people. That day my mind was exceedingly troubled. Some of the children were sad, while others were truly happy at the thought of finally having time to play! Some wanted to know whether they should mark the passing of holidays with drops of mortar or by drawing lines with charcoal. Some were faced with the problem of keeping their eight-page books safe in their houses that leaked in the rain. And others wanted a solution only to the rats that attacked their papers and books. It is difficult to guess why amidst all that significant fuss and clamor Ghisa decided to make himself scarce. That time, as usual, I was unable to track him down. Somewhat worried when I left, my heart was heavy, and my eyes seemed enveloped by fog. In fact, around that time, doctors were beginning to suspect an ulcer in my stomach, and an operation was probable. Fretting over when I would return, or if I would ever return, I cast one final glance, moist with tears, around me. Encountering those dear faces and familiar spaces, my eyes remained glued to them for quite some time.

In the mist that was rising like the earth's breath, most of those uncemented homes had silently disappeared—only the mud-colored straw roofs and the red or black clay roofs appeared to float in the fog like old boats immersed in the muddy water of the rain-flooded River Ganga. In the marshy sand, the melon farms that stretched out far and wide, with their fences made of reeds and their bundles of hay, and the straw huts that had been set up to house those guarding the farms, reminded one of some primitive island inhabiting the sea. In some of the huts, a lamp or two had already been lit when I began to notice a tiny, dark speck far away, moving toward me. It must be Ghisa. . . . I had gauged that from afar. There was no doubt that his young heart had sensed, with all the feeling he was capable of mustering, that today was when he was expected to bid farewell to Guru Saheb. But I had yet to discover the full measure of simple affection, and the extent of anguish at separating from me, that filled that child's heart.

In that hazy dusk, as the bare form of Ghisa came closer, looking like a black sketch on brown paper, I noticed that he was balancing a big watermelon between his hands. It was partially sliced in the middle, and the glowing red interior, amidst the surrounding dark green of the fruit, looked like a partially closed pink flower.

Ghisa had neither money nor a farm—so had he, then stolen the fruit from someone? My suspicion just barely surfaced. And that is when I realized that by creating that feeble, filthy form only to safeguard the pure, gold-like essence of life in Ghisa's person, God was no different from that old man who becomes carefree after burying his gold coins inside a wall made of mud. Ghisa noted that for him, lying to Guru Saheb was the same as lying to God. He had indeed chosen that watermelon several days ago. He did not know why his mother had been held up somewhere, so he had to proceed to the farm alone. There he met the owner's son, who had been eyeing Ghisa's new shirt for many days. Often he would sneer at Ghisa, saying loudly for Ghisa's benefit that "those who serve a platter of food to people whose hunger can be satisfied by eating other people's leftovers are crazy." Now faced with the right opportunity, he had no hesitation in asking Ghisa, "If you don't have money, then why don't you part with your shirt?" And if Ghisa had not acquired the watermelon that day, of what use would it be to him the following day? That is why he gave his shirt away. But there was no need for Guru Saheb to worry, because in the summer, anyway, he does not wear a shirt, and for going somewhere special, his old shirt would be adequate. To ensure that the watermelon did not turn out to be white, he had to have it cut; and to see whether it was sweet or not, it was also necessary to scrape some out with his finger.

If Guru Saheb were to refuse it, then Ghisa would despair and cry all night long—in fact, he would spend the entire summer vacation crying. On the other hand, if she accepted it, Ghisa would bathe every day and revise and master the lessons taught him under the tree, so that after the holidays he would be able to reproduce the entire book on his writing tablet for her to inspect.

And then, keeping my hand on the head of that child who was so resolute in his affection, I stood transfixed and overwhelmed with emotion. That any guru would ever have received such homage from any disciple I find hard to believe. Compared to that extraordinary gift, all the world's give-and-take that had occurred up to then seemed insipid.

Later, having made special arrangements for Ghisa's well-being, I left town, and several months passed before I could return. During that time, it was only natural that no news of him should reach me. When I next found spare time to visit that area, Ghisa's God had permanently relieved him from studying. Today I do not have the strength to repeat that story. But it is possible that as today turns into yesterday, yesterdays into weeks and months, and months into years, I may be able to relate like a philosopher, solemnly and with self-control, the dismal end of that short life. For now, it is sufficient that I continue to search for his reflection in the other forlorn faces I encounter.

*17 August 1936*

# Chapter 8

Like an oil lamp covered by a heavy lid, the lightning had been snuffed out in the sky. The wind had piled one layer of clouds on top of another, giving them scary shapes like night phantom. Soon they became so dense that they looked like a solid black-stone roof dripping with its own moisture.

That day I was feeling somewhat depressed. I was trying, rather unsuccessfully, to forget my pain by resting my head on the table in the small outer room that served as my study. Like an enlarged photograph, the face of a girl who had come from far south and lay sick with typhoid in the student hostel kept magnifying itself between my shut eyelids. Being of modest means, how could her parents possibly afford to come and see her? As I worried about her, my mind became more and more anxious, and my exasperation with myself grew proportionately.

If my body was so pampered that I found it a chore to stay up even a few nights to share the joys and sorrows of the girls put in my charge, how could I justify bringing them over to live in the hostel so far from their mothers? When I myself was still struggling to become a better human being, how could I have the nerve to take on the responsibility for shaping those girls into better persons? Such arrogance, I thought, surely deserves a place in the category of unforgivable offenses.

While I was ruminating in this manner, the sudden sound of someone's footsteps on the veranda outside my room interrupted my train of thought.

After waiting for a couple of minutes for someone to say something, I asked, "Who is there?" In response, a graceful white hand emerged from behind the curtain, moving it ever so slightly. A frightened female voice asked haltingly, "Can I come in?" There was such indifferent politeness in my words—"Please come"—that the feet of the visitor seemed to freeze. But this was only for a moment, because the very next second she appeared like a colored painting on the blue curtain's backdrop.

As though unable to be fully absorbed by the thin, woolen texture of her moss-green shawl, raindrops appeared glued to its surface. Illumined by the light from the electric bulb, they began to sparkle like small diamond chips. Taking the shawl off, she followed my glance to the chair in front of me and sat down. With an element of both surprise and curiosity in my look, I began to search every line of her face for some unknown, mute answer. On the ends of the two or three tiny strands of hair that dangled around her eyes, I could see a few water drops quivering like mercury. Framed by the slightly spotted purple border of a white sari, her fair and charming face appeared to me like a wilted flower. The front of her nose was red, suggesting that tears had been recently wiped away. The corners of her eyelids, too, had become somewhat swollen, perhaps from crying, as a result of which the heartrending anguish in her eyes had become more transparent. Her lips were so dry that each successive effort to moisten them seemed more cumbersome. I myself was very listless, which is why I kept waiting for her to say something. But she only bent her head down further. As a tear rolled down her cheek, sparkling in the light like a luminous streak, it occurred to me that the woman seated in front of me had come to share some undefined suffering. That she had stepped out of her house in such cloudy, rainy weather was proof that her need to see me could not have been postponed for even a day.

Sleepily I must have posed the same old, familiar question that I had asked countless times of others—"How can I help you?" But her reply—"Please give me some work"—woke me up. I became quickly alert. Although pertinent, it would have been heartless in that context to probe her about her prior work experience and capability. However, she proceeded on her own to supply me with the necessary information. She knew Hindi, she explained, and "singing, too."* When referring to the singing, her entire body appeared to shrink before expanding back to its normal state, as though some difficult task had been accomplished.

Her story progressed further. Her husband had been sick for more than a year and a half, and they had spent everything for his treatment. They had sold all of her jewelry, except for her ring, which contained four grams of gold. Since it was her husband's only gift to her, the mere thought of selling it depressed her. And even if it were sold, how long would the amount it fetched last? . . . If she could not find work, she was not afraid of starving or even dying but . . . here her voice choked. Evidently she had practice in holding back tears, even those that hovered threateningly at the edges of her eyes. Quickly summoning a measure of self-control that proved stronger than the force causing her body to tremble like straw, she was able thus to prevent the tearful silence of her eyes from overflowing.

With no appropriate words of consolation coming to my mind, I tried to hide my uneasiness by expressing curiosity

*Singing, like dancing, is considered a prostitute's trademark.

about her parents and in-laws. The woman's entire body stiffened again, exactly as before. Her words, spoken with a slight quiver, left me somewhat startled. Her in-laws were angry, she explained; they were not prepared to admit her to their household, and her husband refused to go there alone. After her marriage, she had cut all ties with her mother, and she believed it would be better for her to die than to accept money or other help from her.

With that annotation I could follow the essential threads of her story: she was the daughter of a mother who is customarily described as a "fallen woman." And without holding an entry permit from society, my young visitor had sought to join the ranks of chaste women. She did not realize that society holds that magic wand with which only the woman whom it touches and declares to be virtuous can have the good fortune of being considered a *sati,* or a pious woman. Women ordered by society to stand outside the row of virtuous women should consider the privilege of being there, for themselves and their successive generations, as life's greatest boon. Society has entrusted women like her with a task that is by no means petty! The right to deify man's image, which is gigantic like God's, is theirs exclusively. If then, out of perversity, they seek to defy social sanctions, their offense is bound to be deemed unpardonable. Whoever devised the concept of heaven also invented hell—along with the system of consigning humans to one or the other. If all the living beings in hell were to run toward heaven, the world would not be able to function for even a day. By willfully transforming their lives, these women threaten to create chaos, which must be stopped, and for which society finds it imperative to punish them. Isn't it customary, after all, for the creator to be overly protective of the integrity of her or his own creation? So it is that, from time immemorial, society has been trying to make these women understand that, barred from the triple epithets of *mother, daughter,* and *wife,* and freed from those three-fold obligations, they can claim for themselves solely one identity: that of woman. And society's well-being is supposedly dependent upon their continuing to experience that unidimensional identity. If they deviate from their assigned roles and begin to appropriate the roles of mother and wife, society will risk a breakdown of its own social order by giving legitimacy to their false claims.

That naive woman who had appropriated wifehood was definitely incapable of understanding society's complex code of ethics. Her questioning glance silently asked me in a terribly pitiful manner, "Am I not pious?" As I sat there, the contrast between our respective situations became painfully clear. On the one hand, here was a woman whose mother had been denied even the right to be a mother. On the other hand, here I am, whose mother, grandmother, and great-grandmother, and all other female ancestors on both paternal and maternal sides have earned the certified designation of pious wives, not only for themselves but also for me. And they have done that by accepting as their sacrament the dirt that washed off from their husband's feet, and some even by entering the funeral pyre while still alive. Throughout my life I have been addressed by everyone as a venerable mother or respected sister. But which unfortunate soul would risk being defiled by calling this woman a mother or a sister? And she wished to know the basis for her being considered impious? Even if she were to immolate herself, along with her rebel husband, how would the impure genes that were diffused into every cell of her blood ever be washed away? Her willful desire to acquire the status of a pious woman and wife would destroy society's caste system, very much like the low-caste Sudra's penance that proved so threatening to society's socioreligious order that Lord Rama himself hastened to behead him.

After arranging for her to be dropped at her residence, as I walked back from the gate my feet stuck to the ground like a magnet to iron. I don't know how long I stayed awake that night mulling over her problem, but no solution occurred to me. Her husband's honor and her own self-respect would not allow her to accept charity, and the mere memory of her request that I give her work brought an ironic smile to my lips. What did she know of all the havoc that her defiling presence could cause?

After two unsuccessful days of trying to find a source of livelihood for her, what I did reveals my total ignorance of human psychology. I would sometimes ask her to copy an article that was of no further use to me; other times I would get her to write a letter that would later add to the prestige of the wastebasket. But burdened with self-consciousness, when her look became even more downcast and her voice fell even lower, I began to understand that she had seen through the charade. When she fully realized that I did not in fact need her work, my courage to carry the charade any further also ended.

After this there was no news of her for some days. I thought possibly her husband's illness had become more serious. During that time, only on one occasion did she accept some help from me, which led me to conclude that she had indeed accepted my friendship for what it is was worth.

Soon days turned into weeks and weeks into months. Then one day I learned from one of her female acquaintances the epilogue to her story. Although much of it can be characterized as hearsay, it touched my heart unlike any other story.

Even with her singular devotion, that accursed woman was unable to save her husband's life. In his final moments, his father did come to see the dying son's face for the last time. But he did not, even unwittingly, cast as much as a glance at the wretched daughter-in-law who had become weak from fasting and from staying awake for several nights. Possibly, in his mind he harbored the belief that it was because of consorting with that indecent woman that his son was compelled to lose his life.

By the time one of the neighbors came and helped to revive her, they had already carried away her husband's body for cremation. Remaining in a stupor throughout the night, she regained consciousness only when she saw her father-in-law packing his bags in the morning. Wiping her tears with the edge of her sari, she asked from behind the door's screen, "What time do we leave?" It seemed to the exalted father-in-law that he had been struck by lightning. When the strength to speak returned to him, he made the cruelest gibe, saying menacingly, "Just take whatever you brought from your house when you stepped out of it and go back gracefully to your mother's or else we will be compelled to be tough with you. After shaming our family, are you not content?"

The woman did not become enraged. She gave no consideration to self-pride or to insult. Begging only for space the size of one's foot in the house of which she lawfully held ownership, she spread out the edge of her sari and spoke humbly, "There are so many servants and attendants in your house. It won't be too burdensome for you to spare me two fistfuls of flour. I, too, will remain there serving all of you." But the father-in-law's response could have shamed shame itself.

This news about what had happened reached me only after considerable time had elapsed. Eventually, when I set out to trace her whereabouts, someone said that she had gone to a widow's home; another said she had returned to her mother.

By and by, after time had already faded her from my

memory, a filthy envelope made it all come alive again. She is well, she writes; she has not forgotten me but does not wish to trouble me any further. She is able to earn something through sewing and knitting; when she is no longer able to do this, she will not hesitate to ask me for help. She also asks when I will open the center that I was intending to set up to teach women like her to earn their livelihood.

And I am asking myself, "Are you proud even today of being highborn? Do you still have faith in the certificates of good and evil issued by society?"

*6 September 1937*

# Chapter 9

Only a metaphysician or a philosopher would be able to discern whether there was any value in the blind Alopi's uneventful life. To me his story has always seemed like one poignant link in the tragic saga of life. Like Alopi, the story of my encounter with him is also uniquely tragic.

It was the beginning of summer. Like an amateur musician, April was trying to drive the world crazy by playing wild notes on its fiery instrument. Because of the heat, my small house seemed to have turned into a potter's rustic kiln. The breeze was so strong that it was constantly blowing the doors and windows open, and they would shut again with such a clamor that the house sounded like a modern-day factory. I was working in a manner somewhat appropriate to the oppressive heat: I was mechanically grading students' test papers—using my discretion, of course, to sift the grains of accuracy from the heap of knowledge or ignorance that had blindly been stuffed into the answer books.

In the process of grading, I began to think about how very strange we are! As it is, although we use such artificial devices as ice, cooling screens made out of scented grass, electric fans, and the like, we are still unable to prevent our brains from melting in this wretched heat. So why do we choose this particular time of year to test the braininess of others? If we had better sense, in all fairness we would not willingly commit ourselves to the injustice of holding and grading annual exams in summer.

Like a tired traveler, the latter part of the day was advancing slowly, even haltingly. It seemed as though my hand and my sight were engaged in a contest to determine which of the two would race first across the pages of the exam books. At such a juncture, almost anyone's arrival adds a touch of annoyance to one's impatience. And if the visitor turns out to be someone who is seeking a favor, the desire to be hospitable quickly vanishes.

After making their unusually dimly lit cabins even darker, all my servants had voluntarily retreated to their quarters, relishing the comfort of their owl-like state. With no one around to answer the door, my first impulse was to stay put. The caller must be punished for choosing to come at an inopportune time, I thought. But the hospitality I am trained to show toward mendicants is so irrational that it verges on blind faith.

All through my childhood—and substantiating her point with endless examples—Mother tried to explain to us this basic rule of conduct: that our hospitality is better tested when some lost, stranded beggar who is stationed at our door stretches his hand out to seek a shred of our mercy than when some distinguished visitor honors our house with his benign presence.

During Mother's lifetime there were innumerable occasions when the lesson she had taught me was forgotten. But ever since I got past the stage at which compliance meant only loss of face, even those lessons that were supposedly forgotten are coming back vividly, along with all their subtle nuances.

Instead of being responsive to my visitor's need, I was thus more concerned about the test of my civility. I found that I had no other recourse but to get up. After calling out several times and failing to draw anyone's attention, the two figures who had been beckoning for someone to come out and meet them began heading toward the shade of the margosa tree, oblivious to the fact that the tree itself had already lost its leaves. Realizing that I was summoning them through totally impersonal modes of address, such as "Hey! You, over there!" and so on, they headed back toward me. Naturally, my curiosity about them grew with every step they took. Using his ragged, long shirt to serve as a reinforced prison around his skeletal frame, which seemed to be rebelling through the protective layer of his skin, and grabbing one edge of a cane to lead the person behind him, was an eleven-to twelve-year-old boy. Having freed his skeletal form as far as possible from the grip of his high loincloth and soiled waistcoat, and groping his way around with the help of the other end of the cane, a blind man was following him.

His head shaking like an inverted pot on a stick as he gently pushed the old man forward, the child, who had the look of an adult, mumbled something. As the old man looked up and folded his hands to greet me, I could not help noticing that his greeting seemed directed to the palm tree rather than to me. For the first time in my life, I found myself at a loss for the appropriate words with which to frame a question and stood speechless before that blind man.

Not surprisingly, the man's clothes were of the color of dust, and his feet were dust-covered as well. Worse, a layer of grime had settled on his short hair, flat forehead, scattered eyebrows, sparse eyelashes, tired eyelids, thin lips, and pro-truding chin in such a way that he seemed like a figure of partially dried clay. Deprived of his eyesight, his tiny eyes were lusterless like soiled glass marbles, which accentuated the impression that his body was lifelessness incarnate. Perhaps because of his looks the tone of his voice unexpectedly startled me.

The life of this stratum of society tends to be like an open book, so to narrate its story from the beginning to the end becomes relatively easy. Such effortless narration is provoked not only by important, but even by petty, occasions. As opposed to them, our increasingly artificial life and the growing complexity of our inner world inevitably leads to inscrutability. It is almost as though our heron-like exterior comes to rely for its whiteness on the fish rotting in its interior—that is, as if our evil inner self is allowed to be projected as virtue. Thus, our comparatively worthless life stories become increasingly incommunicable, and the simple heartrending qualities of joy and sorrow turn lifeless when narrated. We are unable to recount the entangled tales of our lives in a simple, honest way. And when we set out to do so, each and every string of imagination adds further to the complexity of narration, producing the illusion of countless reverberations of truth.

In the blind Alopi's story no psychological complexities surfaced, nor did one uncover labyrinthine problems. Admittedly, from his pitiful garrulousness, it was evident that the gap caused by his blindness was more than bridged by his speech. And although talent was unevenly distributed among Alopi's five senses, their combined impact was fairly even.

Evidently his father hailed from a clan of small vegetable growers. But after a long wait for the birth of an heir, he was compelled to appear in the guise of a supplicant at the door of Goddess Alopi. Known as Alopidevi, the goddess was perhaps like the generous miser who gives charity more to make a name for himself than to fulfill the need of the beggar. That is why even the young human form that emerged as a result of her blessing bestowed on Alopi's parents turned out to be far from perfect: the son she granted in response to her devotee's wish turned out to be blind. Whereas the parents were not so ungrateful as to throw the damaged gift back at the goddess's feet, to publicize her stinginess and to caution other supplicants, they named their blind son Alopidin—that is, "one who is granted by Alopi."

That same Alopi was twenty-three years old when I met him. And his vegetable-grower father, recovering only the interest on the paternal debt owed to him by Alopi, had proceeded to join the ancestral court, leaving Alopi to repay the principal amount through service to his mother. Alopi's mother hawked vegetables for a living. But Alopi felt bad that a young man like himself should sit around idle while the old woman killed herself working. So, having heard about me from his uncle, who was an expert on vegetables, he came to me in search of work.

I had never encountered such a surprising scenario. Admittedly, there will always be youths who, innocent of life's grim vicissitudes, quibble over life's comforts with mothers who work hard to support their families, and whose fingers are pierced from continuous sewing. There is no shortage of young men who, even as they quietly swallow their tears like the proverbial daughters-in-law in a family, are not averse to robbing their poor fathers of everything. And their manhood is neither diminished from exploiting their parents nor numbed from the shameless act of begging. Society is also not bereft of men who, mistaking their failure for success, wrecklessly blow in cinema halls the money painstakingly earned by their wives who labor day-long, leaving their small children unattended.

Generally speaking, for the modern male, valor lies in lamentation. The greater the variety of forms, expressions, and tones with which he is able to sing an elegy to his hopeless life and beat his chest in desperation to announce his helplessness, the more venerable he becomes and the more likely he is to be called a man. In a context where manhood is synonymous with apathy and whimpering, it was unlikely that the industrious and uncomplaining Alopi would find understanding or mercy.

After a while, feeling more at ease, I asked him, "What sort of work can you do?" Alopi had come prepared with his response, having thought it all out beforehand. He would bring in low-cost, good-quality vegetables from the rural farms for me and for the hostel students.

Without giving me the chance to wonder how he intended to take on the sort of responsibility that bordered on an occupation, given his lifelong sightlessness, Alopi pointed to his young cousin Ragghu, saying that with their joint effort, even the most arduous of tasks had previously been accomplished.

Their proposal was unlike any I'd heard before. But I am no less bizarre! Thus, Ragghu and Alopi went away, bearing the massive weight of their new undertaking on their feeble shoulders. The next day at the crack of dawn, grabbing Ragghu's cane with one hand and using the other hand to balance a large basket on his head, Alopi started calling out, "Ma'am! Ma'am! Are you there?"

As time went by, when Alopi began pressing me to find out what I liked, I found myself in a very difficult situation. Some vegetables were excluded from my medically prescribed diet. As for the remaining ones, it was customary that whatever appealed to my maid Bhaktin's discretion be acceptable to me. Moreover, because I was required to live for certain months of the year on yogurt, other months on fruit, and still others on gruel—always a similar soft diet—I could not help treating food preferences indifferently. But so as not to disappoint Alopi, I accepted all that he brought "especially for me." When it came to payment, Alopi said he would collect it at the end of the month. When I spoke to him at length of the possibility of my forgetting to pay and of my indifference to keeping an account, Alopi explained, with supreme confidence, that he would be able to keep accurate accounts for me with the help of his learned uncle who knew tables up to ten and could read the beginner's primer. The account for the hostel would, of course, be kept by its matron.

The uproar that this duo caused among the hostel's inmates was quite amusing. I am unable to describe it, finding myself like the blind or the mute person who is asked to describe what she sees or hears. Yet in just a couple of days, Alopi became the object of everyone's affection. He could take certain liberties that other servants could never expect to take. Settling down in one corner of the courtyard with his legs outstretched, he would proceed to weigh the vegetables he had brought on the big scale, even though he had weighed them once before. His sense of touch had become so acute that merely by holding a squash, a pumpkin, or a jackfruit in his hand, he was able to tell its weight. While weighing the vegetables, he would continue to impart to the cook and her young female helper endless knowledge about vegetable varieties and farming. Usually the younger girls would gather around him and chirp away. In the course of time, he started bringing guavas, plums, and other fruit for them, and I cannot say with certainty about how those were priced. One day the college fruit vendor complained that his business was hurting because of the blind fellow who was bringing fruit to distribute among children for free, and I was forced to confront Alopi. Biting the tip of his tongue and shaking his head, Alopi mumbled something from which I deduced that he did indeed get paid. Moreover, since he did not come during school hours, how could the fruit vendor suffer any loss on his account? Since they could not openly refute what Alopi said without making him appear to be a liar, and they were incapable of telling a lie in my presence, the girls kept mum. Later, in response to my lecture about what is improper and proper, wiping his moist eyes with the dirty cloth that was tied around his waist, Alopi told me that, as his cousin had passed away when she was just eight or nine years of age, the voices of these girls reminded him of her. That was why he brought along the guavas, jujubes, black plums, and whatever else he could afford within his limited means. Back in his village, since no one charged a price for such things, he had no way of knowing that in the city not charging money was considered bad. Had he paid money to purchase the fruit, it would have been appropriate for him to accept payment. But he got the fruit gratis as a bonus to the vegetables he purchased. The mere thought that he should be making money from it made him uneasy. Only after observing the expression on Alopi's upturned face could I grasp the true worth of my fake justice. And then I became impatient with myself. Needless to say, Alopi did not have to change his routine.

Being sightless, Alopi was perhaps neither intimidated by nature's fearsome forms nor misguided by its beauty. When incessant rain would give the illusion of a snowstorm, or lightning would seem like a fountain of flames, or the thundering clouds would generate the impression that the mountains were roaring as the two of them moved about, Ragghu would then seek cover from the elements. But like a drenched, ragged puppet, unconcerned about the water dripping from the tip of his nose, Alopi would walk around, using his wet fingers to grab the slippery cane, carefully balancing on his head the vegetable basket, which seemed like a miniature green farm. He would wade freely through the wet ground as if he were committed to circling the globe that very day. If his feet stepped into a puddle even once, Ragghu was not spared because Alopi deemed such a lapse in guidance by a sighted person to be inexcusable. When the cold weather would weave a sort of phalanx with frosty threads and the wind sounded like the breathing of a person afflicted with palsy, Ragghu would walk around shivering in his thin shirt, his teeth clattering like an epileptic. But shutting the doors to his chilled lips with all his might, Alopi would be seen stepping carefully with his feet, the toenails of which had turned blue, the toes numb from the cold. In the summer, when dust storms appeared as though someone were blowing the earth away after grinding it up and the hot wind ran around screaming from one corner to the other like a person on fire, Ragghu would screen his eyes with his hands and walk fast, his briskly moving feet reminding me of corn popping in an oven. But shutting his eyelids to hold the darkness of his eyes prisoner within them, Alopi would place each foot on the scorching ground with complete patience, as though he were measuring the temperature of the earth's heart. Be it Vasant or Holi, Dushehra or Diwali, or any other festival, there was never a break in Alopi's routine.

On one occasion, ashamed at their long spell of inactivity, our Hindu-Muslim fellow-beings began to engage in an active contest of bravery through religious rioting. At that time, stuffing all kinds of things in his hamper, which by now was twice the size of his first basket, and loading an additional, massive pile of vegetables on Ragghu's back, Alopi managed to come via a deserted route. Instead of surprising me, his bravado made me furious. "You are blind not only in your eyes but also in your heart! By risking your life in those dingy streets during this outbreak of Hindu-Muslim riots, you will not be able to attain heaven!" In response to this and other similar "welcoming" statements, Alopi merely groped silently for the eggplant, squash, and so forth. After placing a mound of vegetables in my courtyard, he set out toward the hostel maintaining that same sort of mute expression. By the time he returned and stood uneasily before me, rubbing his dry eyes, I was no longer upset. Having erupted earlier, my anger had subsided, and my heart was filled with warmth and affection. Sensing a reassuring tone in my voice, he explained haltingly that he had brought along enough vegetables to last two days. Earlier the matron had told him that in the mess store there were no pickles left, and the small, dried lumps of pounded lentils had rotted. Since only people like Alopi can be expected to make a meal of lentils, he had felt compelled to purchase the necessary foodstuff from the rural market and bring it here, somehow taking adequate care to protect himself from the riots. After all, who would really bother to harass a blind man? But since he realized, after coming, that he did not have my permission, he promised not to set foot outside his home. He went on to tell me that there was no need to worry about the vegetable supply for a least two more days, and by that time the communal clash would certainly have ended. Even at such a precarious time it was not possible to ask Alopi to remain back, because the burden of looking after his old mother rested on him.

Being blind, Alopi was unable to see whether I was on the veranda. Yet as he passed to and fro, he would always face the general direction where he thought I would be and fold his hands to greet me.

On countless occasions I had seen Alopi seated beneath the margosa tree with his emptied basket, talking intently with Bhaktin, my maid. The topics of conversation appeared engrossing: whether I like bitter gourd or jackfruit; whether I prefer the buds of the tree *banbinia variegata,* whose flowers are eaten as vegetables, or green beans; whether I relish fenugreek more than spinach; whether sweet lime is more beneficial than orange. These and similar questions would elicit serious debate.

Something happened once, which, however trite, has always seemed profound to me. I was suffering from fever. After greeting my imagined presence on the veranda for several days and getting no response, Alopi said to Ragghu, "It seems this time Guruji is terribly offended. She makes no attempt to talk to us like she used to." But when he learned that I was unable to step out because of illness, he was very upset.

The following day a message came that Alopi wanted permission to see me. Amidst all that suffering I could not help smiling. Even if permission were endlessly granted, how could the *blind* Alopi be capable of *seeing* me! Nevertheless Alopi did come. After greeting me and feeling his way around, he sat down near the threshold. Wiping the moisture from his misty, blank eyes with his sleeve, he undid the knot at one edge of the cloth that was tied around his waist, and he confessed like a culprit that he had personally gone to fetch the holy ash from Alopidevi. If a pinch of it were to be kept on the tongue and another applied to the forehead, the threat of sickness and any other harm could be banished. I felt like saying, "If Goddess Alopi could not make you flawless, what will she be able to do for me?" But the solemnity of her blessing kept me from saying anything sceptical. I should have recognized that to prove the miraculousness of Goddess Alopi, it was enough to have a heart like Alopi's, firm as a rock in its steadfastness to duty, and soft as wax in its tenderness. Alopi's incredible compassion for me whose introduction to him was based entirely on a medley of sounds rather than sight can never be forgotten.

For three years running Alopi had come to us. His almost filled-out skeleton was beginning to be fancily dressed in a shirt; now and then he would adorn his head with a headgear; and the high loincloth that once covered him from the waist down was being tied somewhat lower, making him look more respectable. Ordinarily vegetable purchases each month were in excess of seventy rupees (a little over two dollars). After paying his costs and giving something to Ragghu as well, enough remained for Alopi to be able to live comfortably with his mother. Indeed, one day Ragghu revealed jokingly that cousin Alopi had saved so much money that his mother was keeping it secure by burying it underground!

It seems that God had made all appropriate arrangements to ensure that the concluding chapter of Alopi's bleak life would be no less pitiful than its beginning. One day sitting near me, pretending to talk to herself, Bhaktin said, "Alopi is preparing to settle down." I was so amazed that, forgetting my usual indifference to Bhaktin's gossip, I could not resist asking, "Why?" Bhaktin looked at me with the same elated expression as would have been on the legendary warrior Bhishma's face when he saw the invincible Lord Krishna grabbing the wheel of his chariot in the battlefield and running. I later discovered that every bit of what Bhaktin said was the unadulterated truth.

Hailing from the same caste of petty vegetable growers as Alopi, a woman who had already divorced two husbands had expressed an interest in creating a heaven on earth for the blind man. But Alopi's mother was unwilling to give away in charity the son she had received as a blessing.

Coming back after the summer holidays, I heard that Alopi's mother was living separately, since the assertive bride had come to take charge of the house. Later I also got to see her. She was a middle-aged woman of average height and

build. She seemed quite ordinary to look at. But in her voice
there was such seductiveness and such compelling intimacy
that she could not fail to attract everyone. In her unusually
fiery eyes, along with shrewdness there was a streak of cold-
bloodedness that made it certainly difficult, if not impossible,
to trust her. Alopi, of course, knew her only by her voice,
which is perhaps why he was able to trust her.

Ragghu served as the household spy, and from him everyone came to know that no topic of conversation interested
Alopi's new wife more than money. She would sometimes ask
if Alopi had saved anything for a rainy day. At other times
she would wonder aloud in which corner of the house her
bracelet and earrings should be buried for safekeeping.

Alopi was able to live in that collapsing heaven for barely
six months. Then he learned that his shrewd wife had taken
off with everything, freeing him from her magical hold
forever. Poor soul! For several days he was unable to believe
what had happened. He would grope around for the pit where
his savings had been buried, and then, settling down near the
door, he would sit and wait for her.

When the uncharitable neighbors took every opportunity
to attack him for believing that she would return, he became
heartbroken and fell sick. Yet whenever someone suggested
that he inform the ever-diligent police of the burglary, he
would say, with quiet, despairing resolve, "Only a scoundrel
would try to have his wife caught and summoned by reporting
her as missing and by giving a description of her to the
police."

After he had recovered somewhat, Alopi resumed his visits
to our campus. But he seemed to have lost his earlier vitality.
It was as though there were no life left in him: walking by,
he would drag his feet and his cane would almost slip from
his hand. Once, while folding his hands in the direction of

the veranda to greet me, his basket fell over. Although Alopi's courage, enthusiasm, and self-confidence had been completely swallowed by this single desertion in his life, it seemed more like fiction than fact.

The blind man's pain could only turn mute. Consequently, those wishing to console him found no way to reach out to him. When I would try to discuss what had happened, shame would make him freeze, as though he were being pelted by hail. So I did not deem it appropriate to add to his pain and humiliation by forcing him to talk about it. But the gloomy shadow that was enveloping Alopi began to worry me: he was like a child who, innocent of any wrongdoing, feels speechless at being awarded an unjust punishment.

Out of love for her blind son who had been granted to her as a favor for her penance and devotion, Alopi's mother soon forgot all his misdemeanors. But the stubborn son did not forgive himself. Thus, the sad as well as happy past that had been theirs could not be revived.

I was spending the Dushehra festival holidays at home. One day, after delivering the vegetables, Alopi continued to linger in the mess until evening. Sometimes he would touch the weighing scale with much tenderness; at other times, he would pet the bow-shaped back of the cat with great affection; and at still other times, he would tease the young girls. Later I watched him take out some puffed rice that was tied to his waistband and serve it to my dog, Flora, and next feed radish leaves to Sona, my pet deer. Then he folded his hands generally in the direction of the veranda, where he believed I would be. After this final greeting to me, he never came back.

Three days later, the swollen-eyed Ragghu broke the news that his blind cousin had embarked on a grand journey to some unknown world without taking him along. Since that was precisely how he had first arrived here—unexpectedly and unannounced—I had full faith that this time also he would reach his destination without getting lost.

After arranging some other work for young Ragghu, I put a veil of oblivion on Alopi's remaining relics. But even today, the moment I look toward the doorway, it is as if my vision begins to center in on a shadowy image. Then, slowly, the face of that image crystallizes, and on that face, lusterless eyes appear like marbles made of unbaked glass, and on the sunken cheeks a streak of dried tears is perceptible. Then, rubbing my eyes repeatedly, I think about Alopi, who owed his life to an irony of fate and his death to worldly deception, and I wonder if he will become a spirit that hovers around continually seeking my affection.

*20 February 1938*

# *Chapter* 10

Budloo was as indifferent a manufacturer of his clumsily crafted clay pots as he was a carefree creator of his deformed-looking children. Just as the vibrant coarseness of the inanimate clay with which he molded his pots could never hold his attention, the lifeless ugliness of his living progeny could never break through his ascetic trance.

I saw him constantly surrounded, on the one hand, by piles of clay vessels—baked and unbaked, broken and unbroken—and on the other, by a throng of filthy, naked, emaciated children. Just as the clay vessels would break, partially from drying, baking, and handling, so too the children would pass away: some at birth; others while crawling on their knees; and others as they waddled on their crooked feet, trying to help their parents in their chores. Yet it was never possible to see Budloo either happy or sad in connection with their births or deaths. To profile Budloo would be close to impossible for any artist because he sent out such conflicting impressions that by the time one perception of him could crystallize, the other had faded away.

His face was tawny and gentle. As though rebelling against the constricting hold of his sunken cheeks, the protruding bones on either side of his nose did not fail to make him look like the sibling of a skeleton. His tall, lean body must have been graceful once, but from a lifetime of hand-to-mouth existence it had become bent with the burden of premature aging. His tiny, bright eyes were bashful like the eyes of a woman. But permanently devoid of spirit, they were reminiscent of shells that had been turned into eyes and glued to a statue forged out of oily, black clay. The sound that his crackling throat forced through his trembling lips would startle listeners because it sounded exactly like a conch shell sound emanating from a flute.

By nature Budloo was inclined to speak very little. Moreover, he was unaware of the limited listening capacity of someone "civilized" like me. Therefore, few occasions arose for me to interact with him. Occasionally when passing by, I would pause to look at his still fingers following their routine sequence on the moving wheel, and he would suddenly become embarrassed. Clearing his throat repeatedly to hide his nervousness, he would call out in his jarring voice to Khedan, Dukhiya, Nathu, or any of his other children to bring a chair for me to sit on. As the children would begin the race to bring from the dark cabin the dilapidated, old, three-legged chair with an unstable, sieve-like surface, I would consider departing from the scene an act of kindness to my host. By sitting down I knew I would certainly place that chair in jeopardy. The future of all the clay pots and vessels in the vicinity was similarly at risk. Budloo's house fell along the way of my daily commute, and I was usually in a hurry to get somewhere or back. It was difficult to find spare time to spend there without causing my work to suffer.

On days when I encountered his wife, Radhiya, sieving the clay or doing some other household chore, it would be not only necessary but unavoidable for me to stop for a while. Sometimes through tearful eyes and at others through smiling lips, she liked to relate the story of her colorless life. Her eyes, lips, hands, and feet all seemed eager to narrate their individual tales. While she said very little through words, what she did say was so moving that the listener was unable to quickly regain composure. Like a sad melody, her tale churned the hearts of others as much as it did her own. I often found it difficult to hide my emotions from her.

Radhiya should be described as poverty personified. Tied back with the soiled edge of an old sari, her dry, tangled hair was customarily washed on festive days with black clay. But for lack of means her hair was forever deprived of the grooming touch of mustard oil. The border of her sari was indistinguishable from the rest of the garment because of the grime that had settled everywhere. In fact, the fabric had become so threadbare that when she clasped the upper end of the sari and tried pulling it over her face to serve as a veil, only the border would slip down to her nose.

Because suffering often becomes a sort of ornament or cosmetic, the faces of people who suffer inevitably mesmerize the beholder. The magnetism of Radhiya's face was clearly attributable to her suffering. Otherwise, when examined closely, feature by feature, her face seemed especially plain and broad: her nose, which drew a sharp line between her eyes, seemed to disappear in the region above the lip; surrounded by dark circles, her eyes looked like someone had pressed them down with a finger, burying them in black eyeliner; and her lips were shriveled and stamped with bitterness, as though in continuous contact with a cup of pungent medicine. In that assortment of uneven features, the magnetic harmony that came through must have certainly emanated from Radhiya's anguished heart. As emaciated as she was, squeezed dry of the juice of life, she seemed that much heavier from being drenched in suffering. Perhaps that is why she had neither that vacant look about her that is unable to hold someone's attention nor that superficiality that does not have the power to touch the heart.

Radhiya was certainly unacquainted with any ornament other than her round, metal bracelets, which had become flat with constant wear, and her lacquer bangles, which had lost their shape and shine from so much grime. But she never really noticed the absence of jewelry. Although well-built and rounded, she had been reduced to such a bare skeleton by the unbroken chain of children and the unbreachable shadow of destitution that to see her functioning at all was a source of amazement.

The sort of harsh impertinence usually found in women from this social stratum was altogether missing in Radhiya, which is probably why my indifference inevitably turned into curiosity, and curiosity into respect. Her love for Budloo was sincere and unconditional. Budloo was never known to fret over the house, the children, or her, but no one ever heard Radhiya speak ill of her simpleton husband. Radhiya was confident that her husband was a jewel among potters and a fine artist; people were just unacquainted with his greatness.

Getting up early every morning, sometimes to grind corn, millet, maize, barley, or gram, Radhiya would begin to perform her exacting duties. And her chores would conclude only when, by the dim light of the glimmering oil lamp or by the light radiating from the sparkler-like reeds, the left-overs from the morning meal had been dished out to children who were either sleepy or cranky.

Budloo and Radhiya had five surviving children. But when Radhiya counted their number, she never failed to include those whose existence had become merely a memory. Accounts of the three dead children were so interlinked with the survivors' stories that the listener was compelled to consider them alive. The only difference was that the dead, like the heroes and heroines of stories, were alive in an ethereal or ghostly sense and as conversation pieces, and those who were alive were doomed to die early while assisting their artisan father and laborer mother in their struggle for subsistence. From digging the soil to transporting the clay pots to the market, they put their feeble, naked bodies to just as much use as would give their souls an excuse not to renounce their bodies. However, when even the youngest—four- or five-year-old Nathu, stacking on his head a pot ten times bigger than his potbelly, and walking proudly on his crooked, shriveled feet—would express his eagerness to go to the market, one could neither smile nor shed tears at his valor.

The sale of pottery did not yield enough, and sensing that they were not about to make ends meet solely by their hereditary occupation, Radhiya would work in the neighboring farms. Often, by the time she returned from the farm and Budloo from the market, the little ones, after lying down in some corner of the makeshift terrace or upon the dusty ground, would already have dozed off. Radhiya would then carry them inside, and she would lay them down in a line to sleep on a bed made of an old, filthy, ragged sari. During that transitional process, the one who chanced to wake up was given a slice of coarse *roti* taken from a pot that was inside a hanging string basket. And the ones who continued to sleep had to spend the night being content only with affectionate pats.

Budloo was also a claimant of the sacred contents of that pot. But it would be difficult to gauge how many times this woman—with an infinite desire to feed everyone, like the legendary Goddess Annapurna, but with a finite treasure of food—was compelled to conclude her own fast not with a meal but with sleep.

Those two were strange, indeed. The husband, unable to

provide two square meals a day, was incapable of even clothing the children and did not worry over their present or future, but the wife was simply unable to find fault with him; she could find no reason to be dissatisfied.

At the birth of Radhiya's children, there was never any hubbub. On the night when little Lakkhi was born, I saw Radhiya working until late in the evening carrying a big earthen pot filled with water. Setting the pot down, she took out the familiar old three-legged chair for me. Balancing myself with great caution, I started chatting with the children, and Radhiya began to clean her blunt-edged sickle by rubbing it on a stone under the terrace. I asked in a tone of some amusement and surprise, "To what use is this going to be put tonight? Are you going to slit someone's throat?" In response Radhiya gave a weak smile.

The following day, because of a religious holiday, I had some free time, so I was able to go over and visit. As always, Budloo's pottery wheel was moving indifferently. But surrounding the entrance to the house, children were creating a ruckus. Ignoring the reticent Budloo, I asked Dukhiya about her mother. Being the most talkative of her brothers and sisters, she proceeded, breathlessly, to weave endless tales around what had transpired: "A new brother had been born. Mother did not allow the midwife to be summoned—she wanted to be paid one rupee (3 cents). *Mai* (Mother) cut the umbilical cord herself with the sickle; it is buried in a corner of the porch. The brother is resting with his eyes closed and his feet curled up like a lapwing. *Bappa* (Father) has given some maize bread to *Mai.* . . ." In just a few seconds, all those mighty facts were fed to me. I tried unsuccessfully to peep inside, but in the darkness, wrapped in filthy clothes, the dark-skinned Radhiya had blended with the smokey mud

2

walls. After being invited to come closer to see our future potter, I stepped inside.

Once I was inside the cabin, the pervasive smell of smoke and tobacco started to burden my breathing in a peculiar way. Plastered with yellow soil, and covered with termites that seemed like pox marks, the walls appeared as though they were no longer able to support the heavy roof and were anxious to sit down and recover from their fatigue. In the near corner of the stove, the muddy, black pots in which foodgrain was stored alongside the sparkling plates and cups appeared like a lineup of class A and B (privileged and nonprivileged) prisoners inside the insurmountable walls of a prison. In the middle of the house, the length of the hammock-like cane bed, which was intended for the lord of the house, refused to accommodate the feet of the person who was asleep in it. In the niche of the wall, which seemed like a ditch, a neglected, gray, dusty lamp was keeping an inch-long wick and a few drops of oil saved only to justify its existence.

In the vacant western corner of that home, Radhiya was getting her child acquainted with life—as well as destitution. With his eyes closed, the baby seemed like a wingless chick that had just sprung from the egg of some large bird. Where the cord had been cut, some swelling had occurred, and the blood had clotted. I learned that since the midwife did not agree to drop her price to less than a rupee, and since Radhiya considered it unwise to be wasteful, she took care of the childbirth all by herself.

On account of the pain, it had been difficult for her to get up at all; since the cord had to be cut while she was lying down, it was not properly cut. "But there is nothing to worry about," she explained, "because by applying oil, it will dry up in two to four days." In utter amazement I looked at the peaceful and gentle expression on the emaciated face of that incredible mother.

When I told Radhiya that I was going to get her some soup made of dry fruit and spices, along with some milk, she began to smile with an even more poignant expression. Whatever she said translated into an expression of legitimate concern— after all, how long could I make such a provision for her? Childbirth, it seemed, was something that was certain to last throughout her life.

When I called out to Budloo, who was seated by the potter's wheel with an immutable expression, and ordered him to bring jaggery, dry ginger, clarified butter, and other stuff from the grocer's, it was as if he had been hit by lightning. Dukhiya's mother—that is, his wife—had always led him to believe that just the sight of jaggery made her throw up, and further, that clarified butter gave her stomach cramps. He had always fed her millet bread and thereafter ceased worrying about her.

Looking at Budloo's innocent face, and glancing at Radhiya—who seemed to crumble with the weight of my unjust censure of Budloo—I had no need whatsoever to seek further explanation from that couple. In a flash I understood that whatever Budloo was unable to provide became harmful or taboo for Radhiya. But hiding my divine enlightenment, I said simply, "Whatever the other women eat, Dukhiya's mother also will need to consume—whether she feels like throwing up or experiences stomach cramps."

In that house, just as a child's birth was unannounced, so too would death creep up silently. Once little Muliya tossed about in high fever. When smallpox erupted, her mother placed her on a broken bamboo bed in a dark corner of the house. Radhiya took utmost care to ensure that whatever rituals were within the realm of her belief and capability, including sweeping the house with a lock of hair and offering a sacrament of water to the margosa tree in the name of the Goddess Kali, were observed. But on the fourth day, the sick child took the unfortunate path to heaven. Budloo was especially fond of that poor girl, so when he returned from immersing her in the grave waters of River Yamuna, sensing the secret anguish in his silence, Radhiya concocted a dream sequence. In her dream, she explained, the Goddess told her that she had sent the girl to them for only a limited number of days; now she should be returned. For a simpleton like Budloo, it was inevitable that he would be convinced by that dream. Since the Goddess-Mother herself was eager to take away his Muliya, it was best that she had not been given any medical treatment. Medicines would not have been able to save the girl anyway; on top of that, they would have had to face the wrath of the Goddess-Mother. Moreover, what better fate could that girl have hoped for than to have the Goddess-Mother herself stretch out her hand to ask for her.

One day I gave Radhiya a pithy lecture about telling lies. But wiping her eyes with the dirty, ragged edge of her sari, she gave me an argument that was no less weighty. Her husband is very innocent, she conceded. His heart is so soft that he loses courage over even petty hurts. The family's condition is not such that everyone can get two square meals a day. So she tries to hide from him the small and the big troubles encountered by her and her children. Of course, Almighty God is free to grant her whatever punishment He wishes in the afterworld, but this much is clear: she does not tell a lie to take something away from anyone. Radhiya's response itself became an enigma for me: could one call her lie a lie? And if not, how else could one describe it?

I explained to Budloo many times that if he were to make beautifully engraved ewers and pots for holding water, instead of unshapely clay pots, they could even be marketed in the city. But fixing his glance on the wheel, with a rattling voice, he answered simply that his father, grandfather, and great-grandfather had all made the same sort of pots that he did. He was, after all, just a boorish village potter. He would never be capable of making pottery that could meet sophisticated city standards. I realized it would be a waste of my time to say anything more then.

One day I took along several paintings to a makeshift school, to explain some mythological stories to children who used to come to study with me. The paintings were hardly artistic, but they were decidedly better than the unsuccessful reproductions of Shiva, Paravati, Saraswati, and other Hindu gods and goddesses usually sold in the market. Of Budloo's children, Dukhiya alone was sent to study. Perhaps she had told her father what she had seen. When, forgetting all his reserve, Budloo came running to me, my astonishment knew no bounds. I showed him all the paintings and also explained their meaning to him, simplifying it as far as possible. But, even after that explanation, Budloo remained seated amidst the children. Watching him stare intently at a picture of Saraswati, the Hindu Goddess of Learning, I was compelled to ask, "Do you wish to keep this with you?" Budloo's expression showed some hesitation. He did not know how he could dare to ask for such a beautiful painting! When I sensed his heart's desire and handed over that painting, he became dizzy with joy, just like a child. Several days later I found the painting of Saraswati glued on the shabby door of Budloo's unlit house. And to be truthful, I must confess that I felt sorry for the unfortunate situation of the painting.

On the day of the festival of Diwali, I customarily buy a bunch of toys made of clay. During this festival the skill of clay craftsmen can be easily exhibited, and with the encouragement they receive that day from sales to customers, they can work all year long, enabling their talent to blossom. The modern, "civilized" age has not only snatched away the enthusiasm for our festivals but also arrested the progress and earnings of these craftsmen. Lost in my thoughts that day, just as I reached the large room to decorate it with the newly purchased toys, I heard Budloo's crackling voice outside. As he had never come to my house before, I felt both amazement and anxiety: Is someone in his house sick? Has some sort of calamity struck them? Coming out in the veranda, I saw Budloo standing in his dirty clothes, holding a broken small basket, looking almost bashful. He came forward and set the basket down in front of him. When he removed the piece of cloth that had been covering the basket, I was left speechless. Budloo had brought an image of Goddess Saraswati—painted with white and golden colors. The tranquil countenance of the statue was made even more beautiful by its white clothes, golden hair, a golden stringed instrument, and a white swan with its red beak and feet. From the skill with which every single strand of hair had been crafted, the sculptor appeared to be highly talented. "From whom did you get this?" I asked. I was in no way ready for the reply he gave. Lowering his eyes shyly and stretching out his shriveled, clumsy hands, Budloo said that he had made that image with his very own hands. As that was not easy to belive, I found myself staring first at the statue and then at Budloo. Is this the same potter who, only a year ago, had expressed his inability even to make attractive pots? I found myself saying inadvertently, "You claim you are a crude village potter who finds it impossible to make even engraved pottery. How then can you visualize making a statue like this?" Slowly the truth came out. While staring at Saraswati's picture, the desire to become an artist was awakened in Budloo's heart. To the extent that it was possible, he put his entire skill into resurrecting the beauty of that picture in clay. He had failed many times. But after continually trying, he was finally able, only that day, to make an image that was worthy of being offered to me as a gift.

From then on, as Diwali festivals came and went, Budloo continued to craft beautiful images; many of these eventually ornamented wealthy homes.

It seemed as though the artless Radhiya had remained alive only to see her husband turn into an artist. As soon as his crude pots were replaced by beautiful images, she departed for some unknown world, taking her affection with her.

Budloo felt desolate then, as if he were one of a pair of geese. From dawn to dusk and from dusk to dawn, he would wait for Radhiya to return. As it is, waiting is painful; but when some living person sits down to wait for the dead, who will never return, it becomes even more tragic. The gaping hole caused by the departure of that chronic liar Radhiya in the life of that desolate rustic became glaringly apparent when Budloo smashed a pot on the head of someone who broached the subject of his settling down in marriage again.

The woman is at her truest in the role of a mother, at her noblest when she is maternal, and at her most beautiful when she is expressing motherly affection. When she enters a man's life, equipped with those characteristics, it certainly becomes difficult, if not impossible, to replace her.

Finally, the thirteen-year-old Dukhiya extended her tiny lap to take her father into her care, along with her brothers and sisters. Becoming a split image of Radhiya, she too began to grow by giving of herself repeatedly in looking after everyone.

Two years ago, one of Budloo's maternal cousins, charmed by his artistry, took Budloo and his children to another city, Faizabad. Yet each year on the festive day of Diwali, he did not forget to show up with some image or another. But this year, there has been a break in his routine; Diwali has come and gone, but Budloo has not yet brought me an image. Possibly he left in search of Radhiya. Yet in every corner of my house, the images of Lord Buddha, Lord Krishna, Goddess Saraswati, and other deities remind me of the rural potter who used to manufacture crude pots on an old potter's wheel. And those images seem continually to challenge me with these assertions: "Art is not an ancestral right" and "Imagination is not the bonded slave of only the affluent and the educated."

*17 December 1936*

# Chapter 11

Dressed quaintly in an old, black peasant skirt that was faded from repeated washings and a torn, filthy veil that was wrapped like a belt around her waist, as she held a large sickle in her right hand, Lachhama jumped onto the heap of grass and leaves below and started to giggle. In a mixture of the Pahadi dialect and Hindi, she asked, "Why should you fear for me? Am I civilized like you? I am, in fact, an animal! Consider my hands and feet; just look at the tasks I carry out!" I have no idea why I found this hill woman teeming with uninhibited laughter so irresistible.

Singed with sunshine, her face looked like a raw apple roasted on a grill. Beneath dry eyelashes, her fluid eyes appeared from below to be swimming in a bottomless pool of tears, and from above as though turned dry with the sunshine of laughter!

The blue color that spread across her lips from having to endure the cold became even more visible against the whiteness of her even teeth. The roughness that had begun to show in her feet from walking over hard stones and in her hands from cutting grass and chopping wood day and night was softened somewhat by the dampness of earth and cow dung.

Made of grass and straw, her house, perched high atop a hill, looks like a blister on the mountain's chest.

Since her father's vision was impaired, her mother's arm

was broken, her nephew and niece's mother had departed for
the other world, and even their father had become a recluse,
there was no one sufficiently capable of providing for these
people. And in such wilderness, what sort of work could
Lachhama do to keep so many people alive? Her problem
continued to defy solution. But like the memory of better
days, there was at least a female buffalo: Lachhama would
fetch grass and leaves for her, milk her, make curd, and churn
buttermilk. During the summer she would also plant some
potatoes around the hut. But even with all this, the food
shortage was not overcome! The problem of clothing was not
solved! Continually drenched in her tears, Lachhama's life
story is so burdensome that even the most tireless of storytell-
ers and the most attentive of listeners are hesitant to bear
its burden.

Lachhama's marriage took place in a village about eight
miles away from any signs of civilization. Her in-laws owned
a great deal of land, farmed extensively, and raised a lot of
cattle—in short, there was plenty of everything. But cruel
fate managed to exercise its irony in one subtle way. Although
her husband could in no way be called a lunatic, his mental
development never did exceed that of a child. In such a
situation, the parents-in-law might well have taken a liking
to the wise and hard-working wife of their retarded son; but
for the older and younger brothers-in-law, she could only be
problematic. Her presence made it imperative for them to
look after their brother's property, but at the same time they
also had to curb the temptation to misappropriate it.

Enduring endless cruelty when she did not agree to relin-
quish her rights to her husband's property, Lachhama was
beaten so severely one day that she fainted, was presumed
dead, and was buried in a hole. How she revived, and with
what unbearable torture she managed to crawl out of the hole

and reach another village would defy description. Yet she did not allow a single word to escape her lips about the cruelty of her in-laws because that, in her opinion, would cause her "family's honor to be defiled." In any event, Lachhama was too proud to confess to being beaten and battered. By concocting a story that she had sustained her injuries from an accidental fall from a steep cliff, Lachhama emerged as a person of courage. That perception would have been impossible if the cruel fact that she was beaten had surfaced.

On the way from where she had been left for dead, for three whole days she had had nothing to eat. But remembering it, Lachhama laughed and shrugged it off by saying, "When hunger was excessive, I would make a round ball of yellow dust, toss it in my mouth, and with my eyes shut, I would imagine: 'I ate a *laddu* [round sweetmeat]; I ate a *laddu*!' Afterward I would drink a lot of water and everything would be fine." Realizing that Lachhama had survived an escape from the jaws of hell, her parents sought to punish her in-laws, but Lachhama's vigorous protest managed to avert a clash of epic proportions.

It seems tragedy has settled permanently in this unfortunate woman's shadow. She had barely returned to her parents when, committing her daughter and one-month-old baby boy to Lachhama's care, her brother's wife bade farewell forever. Along with her broken body and shattered fate, however, Lachhama had inherited a generous and stout heart. Relying solely on that, she took up the bittersweet burden of her new commitment. But that poor soul! What did she know of child care? In her neighborhood there were no other infants and thus no mothers who could have nursed the baby; nor was the baby yet capable of drinking milk from a cup. So Lachhama's clever mind devised a novel solution. After much pleading and persuading, she succeeded in getting someone to give her an empty oil bottle, and placing in it a loose, wicklike stopper made of cloth, she fed the child buffalo's milk diluted with water.

The cruelty inflicted on her by her in-laws had reduced Lachhama's bones virtually to pulp. If sitting for even just a short while, she was overtaken by spinal pain, standing continuously would cause a throbbing pain in her knees. But ignoring the pain by staying up through the night and working on her knees during the day, she was able to raise the child entrusted to her care by her brother's wife without anyone's help. And today that infant has grown so big that he follows her everywhere like a pet animal.

When I first encountered Lachhama, the idea of bringing her to my hometown of Prayaag for an education did occur to me. But in response to my suggestion, Lachhama glanced at her dilapidated house and merely bowed her head in desperation. In whose care could she leave so many people if she went away? At that time there was still hope that her brother, although deranged by the loss of his wife, would return to assume his responsibilities. But even after that hope proved to be illusory, Lachhama's radiant laughter did not fade under the shadow of despair. She smiled naively at me and asked what use education would be to someone living in a jungle. She was convinced, however, that in her setting, learning how to climb trees to chop wood and pluck leaves was indispensable. She also believed that after her aging parents were no longer around and the children in her care had grown up, God would see no purpose in letting her remain on this earth. Thereafter, she would definitely be reborn into a new life, during which she would have ample opportunity to stay with me to pursue her education as well as carry out her responsibilities. I found myself tempted to laugh at Lachhama's insane suggestion that if I wished to teach her, at the very least I should wait for her to be reborn. But the incredible determination and the simple faith in the continuity of life after death that are reflected in that suggestion leave me with a sense of awe and wonder.

I have concluded that if the definition of friendship is the free give-and-take of joy and sorrow on an equal basis, then I certainly lack a friend.

To convey my happiness, not only creativity and talent but also the animal and natural world are significant to me, for only after sharing my joy with the natural and animal world do I feel total contentment. As for sharing pain, to pass on even a particle of that as a burden to someone else is not acceptable to me. Reassured by the happiness of others, I tend to distance myself from them; at the same time I am drawn irresistibly to the distressed, with whom my relationship has always been one of motherly affection.

Although Lachhama's hands, which had been scratched by thorny branches, and her feet which had been bruised by sharp stones gave her a tarnished lode, she otherwise sparkled with laughter. The overriding sentiment I felt in my heart for her was solely one of respectful friendship. In her suffering she was neither so helpless nor so lowly that she found it necessary to rely upon my support. And on several occasions, in fact, I found her to be much greater and more magnanimous than I. I also sensed in Lachhama's conduct a parity that was lacking in other hill women. She bridged the gap between us with her easy, affable manner, so that I did not have to make an effort to reach out to her.

Even while recognizing that I was able to eat the choicest foods, she took considerable pains to bring me, on every visit, whatever edibles were available in the jungle. One day she came running, carrying with her some freshly extracted honey as well as the waxy portions of the beehive, and she began to entreat me to eat the honey immediately. Although I am not much drawn to sweets and just looking at honey reminds me so much of honey bees that it becomes difficult to eat, I had to honor her request and taste it.

In the hills countless people tend bees for the honey market. But Lachhama could not afford to buy the wooden box for beekeeping. And unfortunately her own house did not have the sort of walls in which a beehive could have formed naturally. After probing, I gathered from Lachhama that one of the walls of her house had developed a crack, inside which Lachhama wished to house the bees. But why would bees have chosen to nest there? Having waited endlessly, when Lachhama's patience ran out she caught the bees herself to place in the crevice. Having been stung by them frequently, her hands became swollen; on several occasions, disliking their narrow home in the crevice, they flew off, but eventually some largehearted bees obliged Lachhama by settling there. The honey Lachhama brought me was the first honey from their beehive.

In a similar act of kindness, on the day of my departure, Lachhama went on a search to bring me a bunch of black grapes; she had gathered them as a parting gift for me. Likewise, whenever the buffalo would give milk, Lachhama would come running, sometimes carrying milk in a wooden cup, sometimes curds in a cone made of leaves, and sometimes butter on a leaf. Making muddy configurations on the dry floor with her feet, which were wet with earth and cow dung, she would come up to where I was seated and coax me stubbornly to try some. Throughout my youth I lived in a hostel while pursuing my education. During vacations, when I would go home, only mother showed special concern for feeding me. But her fussing over me always seemed like an exception to the rule. Obviously, I am not accustomed to someone making such a fuss over me.

Immediately after completing my studies I assumed the responsibility of looking after countless students. Consequently, there has been a dearth in my life of those who are persistent in feeding or looking after me. Taking away that self-sufficiency that comes with adulthood—which I am accused of and which I suspect I have always had—Lachhama's persistence restored me once more to a state of dependence natural to childhood.

Lachhama was totally sincere in her affection. One day, vexed at finding my writing constantly interrupted, I cautioned Lachhama, "Next time when I come, I will construct my cottage on the deserted peak of that mountain where no one will be able to reach me." Since Lachhama knew what it was like to continually worry about feeding everyone, she realized that the feeding problem is not easily solved and that no work in the world can be accomplished if one has to worry about that problem. Wishing to protect me from the overwhelming burden of making arrangements to feed myself in that wilderness, Lachhama prescribed a remedy that only she could have thought up. It was her wish that I should go live on the high mountain peak only when her buffalo's two-year-old calf turned four and began to give milk. Then the milk from one buffalo could fill the needs of her elderly parents and her brother's children, while the other buffalo's milk could serve my needs. She promised that everyday she would routinely deliver to me a quart of milk, a pint of yogurt, some potatoes, wood, water, and the like. She would not speak or even look at me; she would only deliver the goods to my door and then go back. After I finished writing my *magnum opus* and tired of living alone, when I would feel the urge to call out to Lachhama, she would come instantly, setting aside her many chores. She would personally cart all my belongings downhill—including, if necessary, the roof of my cottage! At the end of making such a grand and generous offer, when the humble Lachhama began to earnestly study my face for a reaction, I was left speechless with wonder. Solitude and wilderness are easily found; to compose voluminous works is also not difficult; but finding an unselfish, loving helper like Lachhama is next to impossible.

Lachhama's contention that she was lacking in fortune but not in brains was largely true.

One day as she watched me make a painting of the Himalayas, she couldn't help saying, "Had I the equipment, I could have drawn the snow perfectly." In a derisive tone I asked, "What all would you need?" I interpreted her response, delivered with quaint gestures, to mean that she would need a big piece of blue paper along with some white and green paint. Spreading her blue canvas across a level rock of some very high mountain peak, she would then spend the entire day sketching the Himalayas, whose appearance varies from upright like a wall to spread out like a roof to domed like an ornate temple. Naturally, the blue paper would serve as the sky, the white would be used to paint the snow, and the green to paint the pine trees. After that lofty introduction to the humble Lachhama's intelligence, I naturally felt surprised: when she found me laboriously painting the blue sky on a white paper, it must have occurred to her to use the blue paper instead!

On further inquiry I gathered that without ever being taught, Lachhama had such a great passion for drawing flowers, leaves, vines, and creepers that she had tattooed not only the walls of her own house but also those of other houses in her neighborhood with red ochre and rice. Her artistic creations may not have had any value at all. But at the same time, it was easy to recognize such creations as the products of a raw, untrained kind of talent, which was further constrained by the lack of appropriate tools.

In a similar manner, by observing others she learned to knit a little; but in the absence of wool and knitting needles, her desire to knit a sweater for her aging father remained unfulfilled. When I learned from others the cause of her disappointment, I did, of course, get her those things. But I had no doubt that had it not been a matter of protecting her father from the cold, she would simply have refused to accept them. While she had great affection for me, using that affection to selfishly fulfill even her smallest desire would never have seemed right to her.

Ordinarily in hill life, the innumerable inconveniences and miscellaneous wants enable the pursuit of self-interest to be manifest in a very coarse and blatant way. But Lachhama's life has been an exception to this rule.

I was compelled to look for tears lurking behind her spontaneous laughter and to trace the causes hidden beneath those tears. But waving aside my concern, Lachhama managed to nix my probing by saying, "We are savages. What can we possibly want?"

Though clean and pure in her heart, Lachhama was forced to have an unclean body. At times even she became exasperated at her own filthiness, saying, "I am so filthy! You should bar me from coming into your house. Just look around and see how the entire house appears sullied with my presence!" Such outbursts were usually directed at herself, and shortly thereafter she would begin to make excuses to me: "My feet, of course, were washed and thoroughly scrubbed just this morning, but from midway, I had to turn back to feed the buffalo. My skirt was cleaned and rid of dirt just yesterday after I pounded it with a small mallet on the washing stone, but a dumb kid wiped his muddy hands on it. The *odhani* [mantle] was washed in the stream only the day before yesterday, but the rope that is used to tie the haystack snapped, and I had to use the odhani to tie it."

At some point in the distant past, Lachhama had owned a wooden comb. After it had been lost, her only recourse was to wash her hair in the mountain spring and simply pull out some of the more tangled hair. Receiving a black comb as a gift from me was an incredible event for her. Stuffing that comb along with the sickle into her waistband, she pranced around from one part of the mountain to another, and under the innumerable waterfalls she could be seen endlessly grooming herself. When I considered the unusual happiness she experienced from her unique hairstyling, it was hard not to shed tears. How is one to characterize the misfortune of a woman for whom—even in this twentieth century, which is flooded with countless toiletries and cosmetics—such a trivial object as a comb is a rarity?

On one occasion I heard some women say that they suspected Lachhama of performing some unspecified voodoo to cast an evil spell on their offspring. When I confronted her, Lachhama explained that she did indeed engage in rituals. However, they were not aimed at the ill-being of their children but of those who might have been casting an evil eye on *her*. In her house she had an old, moth-eaten picture of the Goddess Durga. Morning and evening, she placed embers covered with an incense stick made out of dried, scented leaves in front of the Goddess and prayed that whoever cast an evil eye on her should have her eyes burn to ashes.

It was hardly easy for Lachhama to understand that it was not possible to guard one's own well-being merely by wishing a curse upon others. Nor was it simple for her to recognize that the proof of true well-being was that by merely encountering it, even the worst "evil" eye may become "auspicious." Nevertheless, she was able to grasp the subtle principle underlying my statement. From then on in her prayers and offerings, she expressed wishes not only for her own well-being but also for that of all others.

This daughter of the mountain was as firm-minded as she was fearless. Just as she was able to find her way even in the darkest of nights aided by her sickle, similarly she could remain undeterred amidst the gravest of challenges through sheer determination.

Some years ago, receiving the news that Lachhama was alive, some relatives from her in-laws' side came with her cretin husband to ask her to go back with them. She begged her childlike, simpleminded husband to entrust everything to his brothers and come stay with her. She offered to provide a plastered, painted, clean cabin for her husband, while she herself would sleep in the buffalo's shed. Though she would sleep on filthy, foul-smelling grass, she would borrow from the villagers a cane bed for him to sleep on. Even if she were forced to go hungry, working day and night, she would arrange somehow to feed him. As he was, after all, her husband, she intended to stick by him for life. But she could not possibly agree to go back to his house where his people would kill her; furthermore, without her, her parents, nephew, and niece would most certainly starve to death.

Despite what she said, her relatives would not agree to leave her husband behind, possibly because they had no faith in the trustworthiness of a deceitful daughter-in-law who was suspected of having magically risen from the dead. Lachhama's attitude caused a wave of dissatisfaction in the neighboring areas, and she became the target of all kinds of rumors.

Society's psychology in the rough terrain of the mountains is no different from what it is in the plains. The mere thought of injustice against a man makes the entire male fraternity eager to take revenge on a woman, but even after receiving proof of the cruelest injustice inflicted on a female, women collectively are not satisfied until they manage to make the unjustified, initial sentence even more punitive. Thus, the situation of the woman who does not seek out the help of a man at every step is unusual. The more she defies his grasp, the more exasperated he becomes, and often that exasperation turns into false allegations. That male tendency is only natural—after all, we are content only when we can prove we possess something that was considered unattainable; there is no need to prove possession of what one already has.

I find it hardly surprising that a person who is standing will consider the effort to stand wasteful when she is told repeatedly that she has fallen! Until a woman becomes so determined and so self-confident that she remains unshaken by the news of her false defeat, she is likely to remain vulnerable.

In Lachhama I saw an unwavering strength but also the generosity to forgive even the cruelest treatment. She neither demeaned herself by being critical of others nor revealed a lack of self-confidence by trying to justify herself to others. Her mirrorlike mind was itself a proof of its purity. In fact, on one occasion, while a gentleman was seated in my house recounting fictitious allegations against Lachhama, she stood outside the door and made faces at the gentleman like a small child. Similarly, whenever our conversation would drift to the village's worst scoundrel, she would simply say, "Let him be." In her self-created dictionary that meant, "Let it pass; he will reap as he sows."

When passersby would treat the grazing buffalo and the shepherding Lachhama with equal contempt, she did not take offense. On the contrary, she would justify their behavior by saying, "We country people are not civilized. We are savages.

And they are so refined. So how can they speak to us? I don't bother to speak to them either. By choosing to talk to me, you are not behaving appropriately. But since you talk so nicely, that is why I stick around you." To grasp fully what is implicit in such broken and segmented statements may not be easy. But this much is easily understood: in her heart, which was cramped by its own modesty, there was no room to harbor ill-feeling toward anyone.

The day of my departure was a terribly painful one for Lachhama. Soon after milking the buffalo, she came running to my house. After fetching and storing water, she made another round. And when the children were fed, she called on me once again. As my packing progressed, it seemed that all the joints in her body had become weary.

It was customary for her to escort me for the first mile. When the milestone for the second mile appeared, I asked her to go back, but she continued to follow me with her eyes, looking somewhat lost and wiping her eyes repeatedly. The paths in the hills are not like the broad, straight roads in the plains. You barely walk four steps before you need to turn right or left; sometimes a tree blocks your vision; at other times some part of a rock obstructs the view. But even after I was no longer visible, Lachhama's choked voice continued to be audible for quite a distance: "Go carefully! Come back soon! Okay? All right?"

Nowadays the question of Lachhama's starvation does not arise. The apple orchards are loaded with fruit. The raw, sour apples that fall from the trees either rot or dry up, and no one objects to their being taken away. These days, sitting beneath any tree, Lachhama forces down her throat one or two pounds of sour, nearly inedible apples. Afterward, without eating anything else for two days or more, she buries herself in work.

But slowly the winter weather is coming, when, like a

painful burden on the earth's heart, as much as three feet of snow will settle on the ground. Then, warmed by the fire's heat in their homes, people will narrate old tales in a new way. And the wealthy and poor alike, secure in the knowledge of their stocked grain, will ignore the wet, cruel pranks of nature. Likewise, many of the animals will be shepherded down to warmer villages at lower altitudes and will be given hay to eat in the safety of their warm sheds. I shudder to think what Lachhama will do then to save herself, her disabled parents, those dependent children, and the unprotected animals from the cold!

That I do not receive any news of Lachhama is both true and false. Once Lachhama heard me say that if she were literate, it would be easy for us to communicate through letters. With broken gestures Lachhama answered in some gibberish, "Of course, I am able to write a letter, but in my own way. Sitting on a rock, I imagine that I write this or I write that; this part is nicely written or that isn't. When it feels as if the letter has been dispatched, then I get up, happily, to cut grass and chop wood. What I write, doesn't it reach you?"

Who can help smiling at the reference to a letter that is written without paper, pen, or the alphabet and is dispatched without the help of the post office? Yet in wintertime, leaving behind the warmth of my rooms in the plains, when I suddenly begin to think about leaving for the mountains, which are smothered with snow—or in summertime, disregarding the beauty of the mountain resorts enhanced by the congregating elite, I become restless to reach the desolate corner of that frosty peak that is silent with pain—then who can say that Lachhama's letter has not reached me?

*28 August 1939*